"I give you a new command: Love one another. Just as I have loved you, you are also to love one another. By this everyone will know that you are my disciples, if you love one another."
(John 13:34-35)

CARING

The iCare Revolutionary Sunday School and Bible Study Method

With great appreciation, I dedicate this book to the many Sunday school teachers, pastors, and disciplers who taught me to love God, others, and myself. It was not with empty words but with living examples that they communicated, "I care!"

With much love, I dedicate this book to my wife, Yvonne, who enlarged my understanding of love. Her love for me and our family over the years has clearly spoken, "I care!"

With the living sacrifice of my life, I dedicate this book to my Savior and Lord, Jesus Christ, who died for me on the cross. His extreme demonstration of love in life, death, and resurrection has shouted, "I care!"

May this book lead each of us to join Him in saying, "I care!"

CARING

CARING FOR MEMBERS AND FRIENDS
IN SUNDAY SCHOOL AND BIBLE STUDY GROUPS

DARRYL WILSON

We enjoy hearing from our readers. Please contact us at www.anekopress.com/questions-comments with any questions, comments, or suggestions.

Cover Designer: J. Martin
Proofreader: R. Clark

Aneko Press

www.anekopress.com

Aneko Press, Life Sentence Publishing, and our logos are trademarks of
Life Sentence Publishing, Inc.
203 E. Birch Street
P.O. Box 652
Abbotsford, WI 54405

RELIGION / Christian Ministry / General
Paperback ISBN: 979-8-88936-242-5
eBook ISBN: 979-8-88936-243-2
10 9 8 7 6 5 4 3 2 1
Available where books are sold

CONTENTS

INTRODUCTION

D o you care? Your actions speak louder than your words. What do your actions show about your love for God? members of your Bible study group? friends beyond the walls of your church? What would others say about you and your care? Would they have stories to tell about your care? As a result of your care, would friends and people in your community be able to tell that you are a disciple of Jesus?

Are you leading your Bible study group to care? Are you leading group members to care about God and those for whom He cares? Are you leading your group to care for each other, for friends, and for people in the community and the world? Consider these words from David Francis and Ken Braddy in *3 Roles for Guiding Groups:* "Your group is more than an assembly that meets for Bible study. It is a flock you care about between group meeting times" (p. 23).

I authored this book to help, encourage, and challenge leaders, care teams, and group members of adult and student (teens) Bible study groups as they express care. The goal is for every group member to say in word, action, and life, "I care!" For some, that will require adjustments. The effort is worth it.

As you read the pages that follow, I use the word *friend* to refer to FRANs (Friends, Relatives, Associates, and Neighbors). *FRANs* is a term used by Elmer Towns in *FRANtastic Days: Reaching Your Friends, Relatives, Associates & Neighbors for Christ.* I invite you to turn to chapter 17 for an explanation of why I believe *friend* is a better term to use than *prospect.*

To distinguish between love as a feeling and love as an expression or demonstration, I will use the word *care* in this book to refer to the latter: love in action. The chapters that follow offer help in understanding why our care matters and how we can move forward in expressing our care for God, each other, and friends.

Interspersed throughout the book, I share testimonies and statistics from 168 Bible study group members who responded to a "Strengthening Care Survey" conducted prior to writing this book. At the end of each of the nine sections of the book, I share reflection questions to use for self-assessment or for discussion and planning with your group or care team. As we begin the journey, may the results be love and care that looks just like God's. May everyone join us in saying, "I care!"

SECTION ONE: I CARE BECAUSE HE CARES

Mike ran into Buster in the church hallway before worship. Buster is the person who enlisted Mike to lead a Bible study group.

Mike said, "Buster, honestly, I don't know what I am doing. When you enlisted me, you mentioned *care*. Can we meet tomorrow so you can explain why care is important and how it can help?"

After ordering lunch the next day, Buster began by saying, "Mike, care is critical for discipling and growing a group. In John 13:34-35, Jesus said, *'I give you a new command: Love one another. Just as I have loved you, you are also to love one another. By this everyone will know that you are my disciples, if you love one another.'*"

Mike said, "So you are using *care* as a substitute for *love*?"

Buster replied, "*Care* is expressing love. How can others know we love them if we don't act it out? Jesus commanded us to love one another like He did. He taught and showed us how to care."

Mike said, "And *'one another'* would be His disciples – us. But how will caring for each other help us reach *'everyone'*?"

Buster smiled. "Mike, you're getting it. When we care for each other, the world will pay attention because our care will look like Jesus. And that love will attract them to Him. So, your job is to lead your group to love like Jesus."

CHAPTER 1

GOD AS SHEPHERD

On the pages that follow, when I refer to Bible study groups, I include both small groups and Sunday school classes (whether at home, church, or another location). Care is essential in every setting for groups. As you read, consider the sheep God has entrusted to your care.

There are scores of times in the Bible where God is referred to as a shepherd. We find references to a Shepherd-God in Genesis, 2 Samuel, 1 Chronicles, Psalms, Isaiah, Jeremiah, Ezekiel, Hosea, Micah, Zechariah, Matthew, Mark, Luke, John, Acts, 1 Peter, and more. The original hearers understood this image well.

Jesus took up the shepherd image in the fourth of seven *"I am"* statements in John where He says, *"I am the good shepherd. The good shepherd lays down his life for the sheep"* (John 10:11).

Keep in mind God's reply to Moses' question about His name: *"I am."* For the fourth time in the Gospel of John, Jesus uses that most sacred name to refer to Himself. Jesus is saying that as God, He is the Good Shepherd, the Shepherd-Owner, who lays down His life for the sheep. He bought and paid for them in full with His blood on the cross. This was the ultimate display of His love, of His care, for the sheep. He who was without sin died to pay sin debts that none of us could pay.

Sometimes we forget an essential truth: The sheep in our care don't belong to us, they are the Lord's. We care for sheep that belong to the most important person in the universe: God. His ownership increases the importance of our stewardship of them.

When we protect and care for the sheep (the people in our groups), we are caring for His sheep. A steward is someone who is given responsibility for something that belongs to someone else. We are shepherd-stewards of His sheep. When we fail to care for the sheep, we fail to provide the care He desires for His sheep. In fact, Jesus illustrated that very fact in the next two verses: *"The hired hand, since he is not the shepherd and doesn't own the sheep, leaves them and runs away when he sees a wolf coming. The wolf then snatches and scatters them. This happens because he is a hired hand and doesn't care about the sheep"* (John 10:12-13).

WE ARE SHEPHERD-STEWARDS OF HIS SHEEP.

Jesus is making two clear statements. Those charged with protecting and providing care for the sheep: (1) are not providing care because (2) they don't care for the sheep. These are essential lessons for us to learn as His shepherd-stewards. Jesus expects both: caring action and caring relationships.

CARING ACTION AND CARING RELATIONSHIPS

In the original language of the Great Commission (Matthew 28:19-20), Jesus commanded us as His disciples: As you are going, *"make disciples of all nations, baptizing them . . . [and] teaching them to observe everything I have commanded you."*

As we are going at home, at work, at school, and in the marketplace, He commands us to make disciples by leading people to faith in our Lord Jesus and teaching them to obey Him. To obey His command, we interact with and provide care for people along our journey. We develop relationships and display care because Jesus cares. As we are going, our words and actions allow us to demonstrate, "I care because He cares."

In Section One, the focus is on *why* we care. The chapters that follow Section One provide answers to *how* we care. I share practices for how Bible study groups can provide care for members, absentees, and people in our community and the world (friends). Keep in mind that people don't want to be our projects, they want to be our friends.

When we have not previously established caring relationships, it is sometimes necessary for us to begin by acting out that care. Words are not enough. Because it is true that people don't know how much we care until we show them, I encourage you to think of each practice shared as opening the door to ongoing, ever-deepening caring relationships.

HOSPITALITY

As the body of Christ, we have opportunities to extend hospitality. In His earthly ministry, Jesus depended upon the hospitality of others. It should not be surprising that hospitality is an expectation that Jesus has for His people. What is biblical hospitality?

> THE GREEK WORD FOR *HOSPITALITY* USED IN THE NEW TESTAMENT IS *PHILOXENIA.* IT IS ABOUT BEING A FRIEND TO STRANGERS.

I experienced that kind of hospitality in Israel when my touring group entered a Bedouin tent. The Bedouin family welcomed and fed us while they patiently explained their lifestyle and ways.

Hospitality should also be a customary practice for Christians. In Romans 12:13, Paul writes, *Share with the saints in their needs; pursue hospitality.* While we expect to practice good with our friends, I find it fascinating only seven verses later that Paul writes, *But if your enemy is hungry, feed him. If he is thirsty, give him something to drink. For in so doing you will be heaping fiery coals on his head* (Romans 12:20).

Paul challenges us to practice hospitality even with our enemies. Wow! Consider this. How will those who do not know Jesus come to know Him if we never show them the difference He has made in our lives? Caring like Jesus is unique and attractive.

The bottom line is to be a caring friend. But instead of only being reactive, also seek out opportunities to live like Jesus and love people like Jesus does. As you do so, keep in mind that God is the audience for our care. Consider this verse: *Don't neglect to show hospitality, for by doing this some have welcomed angels as guests without knowing it* (Hebrews 13:2).

CHAPTER 2

WHY WE CARE MATTERS

Jesus, the Good Shepherd, knows all about love. He told us as His disciples, *"I give you a new command: Love one another. Just as I have loved you, you are also to love one another. By this everyone will know that you are my disciples, if you love one another."*

LOVE LIKE JESUS

What is new about this command from Jesus? The newness comes from Jesus' example: *"Just as I have loved you, you are also to love one another."* Jesus' life and teachings showed the new, revolutionary difference in the love He commands. He taught us as His disciples to turn the other cheek, go the second mile, and love our neighbor. He cared for many who were overlooked in His day: the leper, Samaritans, the authorities, the blind, the sick, the poor, children, women, and more.

And as the ultimate demonstration of God's love for us and the world, Jesus expressed His love all the way to the cross: *But God proves his own love for us in that while we were still sinners, Christ died for us* (Romans 5:8).

Without hesitation, *We love because he first loved us* (1 John 4:19). The demonstration of His love for us is the *why* and *how* for our love. It is the motivation and example for our care.

LOVE IS A COMMITMENT AND AN EXPRESSION

Our relationship with God connects to our practice of love. Love is more than a feeling. It is commitment and expression or action. When we examine His words, Jesus wants *everyone* to know that we are *His* disciples. And we can best express this through our love toward Him, each other, and ourselves. Doing so sounds like the Great Commandment: *He said to him, "Love the Lord your God with all your heart, with all your soul, and with all your mind. This is the greatest and most important command. The second is like it: Love your neighbor as yourself"* (Matthew 22:37-39).

Practicing love (care) is a choice, not a requirement. It is a decision to express our love for Him. It expresses our faith and love to Him and others – and even ourselves. To distinguish between love as a feeling and love as an expression or demonstration (love in action), I will use the word *care* in this book to refer to the latter: love in action.

LOVE AS A COVENANT

Day 40 of *The Love Dare* book by Alex Kendrick and Stephen Kendrick is entitled, "Love Is a Covenant." It compares contracts with covenants. They explain the differences this way: "A *contract* is usually a written agreement based on distrust, outlining the conditions and consequences if broken. A *covenant* is a verbal commitment based on trust, assuring someone that your promise is unconditional and good for life" (p. 196).

Many approach their relationship with God more like a

contract than a covenant. God's love for us, however, does not change. It does not necessarily depend on our practice, but yet the world cannot see what we do not practice. Our caring practices can also be a means to open our own awareness of His love when we feel unloved and unloving.

My wife and I have celebrated many Valentine's Days together. She knows I love her, but I still need to show her. I give her flowers, cards, and gifts. I take her to a nice restaurant. It is a time for us to *practice* the expression of our love. She knows I love her, and I know she loves me. But love is more than knowledge and feelings. It is a choice, an opportunity to express our care.

MAY EVERYONE BE ATTRACTED TO OUR GOD OF LOVE.

In the same way, we have many opportunities daily to express our care for each other and for *everyone*. When our love resembles Jesus' love, then *everyone* will know we are His disciples. May our words and actions say, "I care!"

So, love God. Love your spouse. Love one another. Love friends, relatives, associates, and neighbors. Love your world. Care for them and invite them to your Bible study group. And may everyone be attracted to our God of love. May they desire to know Jesus.

CHAPTER 3

ADDRESSING NEGLECT OF CARE

John was clear about how much God loves you, me, and the entire world: *"For God loved the world in this way: He gave his one and only Son, so that everyone who believes in him will not perish but have eternal life. For God did not send his Son into the world to condemn the world, but to save the world through him"* (John 3:16-17).

When God gave Jesus, He spread his arms apart as far as the east is from the west (Psalm 103:12) to allow *everyone who believes in him* to set aside the sin penalty we all deserve (Romans 3:23) and to have a restored relationship with God who is love. That extreme demonstration of love is the motivation for our care.

Despite the clarity of that display, however, sometimes distance creeps into our relationship with God. No, God does not move, we do. When our love for God grows cold, apathetic, or distant, our care for our world and even ourselves suffers. For the Christian, this may be the number-one reason we neglect care. Let's examine reasons why this may happen.

REASONS FOR DISTANCE

Ideal care in human relationships is organic and spontaneous. No planning or organization is necessary. But relationships are often messy. Sometimes, messiness requires intentionality in fighting interruptions, obstacles, and poor habits.

In a similar way, when distance arises in our relationship with God, it helps to examine and address reasons why this may have happened. Early hints of that distance become visible in our lack of care for others, ourselves, or the world. Pay attention. His love connects directly to our care.

What are reasons why neglect may creep into our relationship with God? Consider these reasons and solutions:

1. LACK OF A FRESH RELATIONSHIP WITH GOD. One week or one day without a fresh relationship is too long. Fresh means today, now. Fight drift by listening to God in His Word. Spend time with Him daily. Make a commitment. Set appointments to meet God in Bible study – and keep them. Read the Word. Meditate on it. Memorize, apply, journal, and live it. Practice spiritual disciplines. Listen to His still small voice. God speaks a life-changing word to us every time we open the Bible. Recognize the presence of a big God and value His words. Recognize His purpose in speaking to us – we need change. Understand He wants good for us even if change brings pain. He loves us. Find the best time and method, but keep it fresh.

   SOLUTION: Listen to Him speak when you read His Word.

2. LACK OF UNDERSTANDING OF GOD, THE WORD, HIS LOVE, AND OUR MISSION. Today there is much biblical illiteracy. A fresh relationship with God sends us to the Word, which leads us to understand Him, His love, and our mission of care. Nothing substitutes for spending time in His Word. No one can do it for us. As our understanding grows, we

walk in awe that He loves and includes us. We care for others not out of duty, but as an expression of our gratitude and love for Him.

SOLUTION: Read His Word daily for greater understanding of the One speaking and His commands.

3. SIN. When we choose any other way than God's way, we sin. Sin darkens the reflection of God in us. It causes less of His glorious light to shine from our lives. As a result of sin, our mind, attitudes, and actions fail to look like Him and His love. Suppose a young-adult leader announces he is moving in with his girlfriend and leaving his group. When asked about his decision, he acknowledges that it is sin. You see, sin is the result of us caring more about self than about God, His ways, or others and their needs.

SOLUTION: Spend time daily in Bible study and prayer, allowing God to identify and root out sin in your life.

4. PREOCCUPATION. For this discussion, preoccupation is focus and thought engrossed in anything other than God and His mission. We can direct preoccupation toward positive or negative things. It can be food, money, family, pleasure, recreation, work, and more. These can become bad when our priorities and busyness lead us away from God and His mission. Our preoccupations rush to fill all available time and attention, unless we intentionally commit the time to God and to caring for His sheep.

SOLUTION: Reflect daily on how you invested your time and attention. Ask for His help to follow where He leads in every interaction and decision.

5. PERSONAL STRUGGLES. Each struggle is an opportunity to seek God and His ways in it or to be consumed by it. Are you experiencing fear, stress, emotional issues, or

difficult circumstances? When we are hungry, it is difficult to focus on anything else. I have learned through fasting, however, that even hunger can give me a heart of gratitude for all of God's provisions. During struggles, ask for His help. Recognize His presence and blessings even in difficulty.

SOLUTION: Ask these questions: What help has God offered? What does He want me to learn? How can I trust Him more and care for others as I walk through this struggle?

Has neglect in your relationship with God impacted your care for others? If so, the first step is to acknowledge that fact and confess it. Seek Him. Ask for His help. Spend time in His Word and in prayer. Listen to what He has to say and follow where He leads.

Jesus died on the cross to pay the sin penalty for each of us. If you need a relationship with Jesus, ask His forgiveness for your sin and ask Him to give direction to your care and everything you do. Today is the day.

Each of us needs a fresh, daily relationship with our Lord. My friend Dwayne McCrary wrote a brief but important book entitled *It Begins With Prayer.* On page 10, Dwayne writes, "Another interesting fact about sheep is they need to eat every day. One way a shepherd knows a sheep is sick or in distress is by observing its eating habits. Healthy sheep need and want to eat every day. Believers also need daily spiritual nourishment."

EACH OF US NEEDS A FRESH, DAILY RELATIONSHIP WITH OUR LORD.

As His sheep, each day we need to feast on His Word. Out of a daily, fresh relationship with God in Bible study and prayer, we can care for others in ways that honor Him and say, "I care!" In the following chapters, I will focus on relationships and expressing care through the Bible study group. Keep in mind the goal of caring relationships along with caring actions.

SECTION ONE: I CARE BECAUSE HE CARES

REFLECTION QUESTIONS

1. CHAPTER 1: How does John 10:11-13, 16 relate to caring for members and friends?

2. CHAPTER 1: What was the definition of *hospitality*? How does hospitality relate to our work of care?

3. CHAPTER 2: What is new about Jesus' command to love one another? How should that newness impact our care?

4. CHAPTER 2: *Care* in this book refers to the expression of love. Why do our words need expression?

5. CHAPTER 3: Of the five reasons why neglect may creep into our relationship with God, which one has been more of a struggle recently? What step(s) can you take to address that neglect?

6. CHAPTER 3: In the quote from Dwayne McCrary about sheep, how does his quote relate to care for God and others?

SECTION TWO: ORGANIZING FOR CARE

Three months later, Buster invited Mike for breakfast at McDonald's. After they had eaten, Buster asked, "Mike, how is leading your group going?"

Mike said, "Good. As you know, this month we had eight or nine each week. I've been working on care since we talked. We had a cookout. I visited a couple of absentees and a couple of new people. And we plan to help with the church's block party. But I'm getting overwhelmed. Care is more work than I expected."

Buster said, "Mike, that's because you are doing it all yourself. You need help. Pray to the Lord of the harvest to send workers. And then look for those He sends."

Mike said, "I can do that. But for which workers do I pray?"

Buster said, "Because the span-of-care ratio is one caregiver for every five members, you already need help. Start by praying for care team members. I will send you suggested job descriptions."

Mike asked, "And then what?"

Buster said, "When God lays someone on your heart, ask them to help you in areas where care is needed. Work together, and when they are ready, invite them to join you as part of the care team."

CHAPTER 4

THE CARE TEAM

Section Two focuses on two essential areas of organization for care: care team members and enlisting the team. I share job descriptions for Sunday School classes in Appendix 3A and small groups in Appendix 3B. Before reading further, review the job descriptions that apply to your group setting, and then turn back here to see ways care team members interact. Beginning with the care team helps the chapters that follow make more sense. When implemented, this team lightens the care load for the group's leader.

Is your adult or student (teens) group organized to care for members, absentees, and friends? Does your group have an intentional plan for developing healthy relationships and for caring in times of need?

Do you have a plan for communicating discovered needs? Does your plan include steps you will take to address the most common needs? How do you contact group members, absentees, and friends about plans for socials, projects, and meals?

How quickly can you mobilize communication and ministry? Who is keeping the contact list up-to-date? Who will take which action? Who will lead the plan? If no one is in charge, there is no plan, and relationships and ministry in time of crisis will falter.

You don't need to do this work alone. Invite others to join you in saying, "I care!" Your group's care team will help address each of these questions and more. I address team enlistment in chapter 5.

CARE TEAM JOB DESCRIPTIONS

The job descriptions shared in Appendix 3A (Sunday School classes) and 3B (small groups) focus on relationship development and care. Care team members may naturally serve in additional ways not listed, such as teaching and disciple-making.

THE POINT IS TO MAINTAIN THE FOCUS ON RELATIONSHIPS AND CARE.

Consider these job descriptions to be idea-generators for developing your own. If you don't like the titles, change them. If you need to add something, do so. Work to keep job descriptions simple but clear. The point is to maintain the focus on relationships and care.

WORK TOGETHER AS A CAREGIVING TEAM

There are three key reasons for leader failure in carrying out job descriptions: (1) the wrong person was enlisted, (2) the duties in the job description were not explained, and (3) no one encouraged the leader while carrying out the work. To avoid leader failure for these reasons, leader encouragement and enlisting leaders the right way are essential.

I will share about enlistment and explain tasks in the next chapter. As far as positive accountability, you will seldom experience failure to carry out job descriptions if you do the work together. Be a cheerleader and a partner for your leaders as you say together, "We care!"

As you read through the job descriptions, I am sure you

noticed the many ways these care team members work together. Allow me to point out a few of those ways.

- LEADER AND APPRENTICE LEADER. They enlist, train, lead, plan with, encourage, and assist the group's care team with individual and group plans.

- SOCIALS, PROJECTS, AND MEALS. While we may occasionally plan one of these events only for members, our Lord's love encourages us to include friends. That means that care team members will often partner on these events for planning and communication.

- RECORDS. Often group members will have the most frequent contact with other members, absentees, and friends. As a result, they will communicate contact-information changes and caring-contact reports to the care team as appropriate.

- MEETING NEEDS. Any group member or leader may discover the needs of members, absentees, or friends. When a member discovers a need, the member handles the need or informs the care team if the need is too large. The care team handles the needs that they can. If they cannot, the care team shares the need with the group. If the need is larger than the group can handle, it may be taken to the pastor or the church by the group's leader.

- GREETING. The care team leads the entire group to welcome members and guests. No member or guest should enter without warm hospitality from beginning to end of group time and group events.

- GUEST REGISTRATION. The group seeks guest contact information and passes it along to the care team. That information enables the care team and the group to provide ongoing, caring follow-up.

- SETTING GOALS. Goals for caring contacts and disciple-making benefit from input of all care team members. Planning, communicating, and events need the strong relational components that are the focus of these team members.

- RELATIONSHIP DEVELOPMENT. When the work outlined here is carried out, relationships between care team members and with group members and friends will grow stronger. Interaction will be consistent and caring. That care will attract new people to the group and to the Lord.

This is only a starting list of the many ways the care team and group work together. When the teacher or leader and apprentice lead, support, and encourage this caring work, group growth is inevitable. As you can see, the work outlined here is beyond the ability of one leader alone.

When we gather a care team around a leader, the span of care multiplies. Each care team member added enables the group to care well for up to five more people. Even in the smallest group, the leader will want to enlist one team member, and even more as the group grows. More on enlistment in the next chapter.

CHAPTER 5

ENLISTING THE TEAM

Chapter 4 and Appendices 3A and 3B outlined the work of the group's care team. It is essential for adult and student groups to enlist care teams. Let's look at places where care teams have an impact: the group, the church, and the world. Then we will examine *how* to enlist care team members.

THE GROUP

Care teams help the group expand care beyond the ability of the leader alone. They add relationships, experience, creativity, and time to the ministry of the group. Care team members connect with members and absentees to help them to stick and stay. The team leads the group to maintain a focus on people in the community. They discover needs through interactions and enable the group to mobilize to meet those needs in a timely fashion.

THE CHURCH

A few years ago, the church expected group leaders to surround themselves with a leadership team. The church and group leaders trained these team members and led them to serve in the safe environment of the group. And because of serving in the group, members of the leadership team discovered abilities and gifts needed in other ministries throughout the church: committees, teams, deacons, younger-age group ministries, and more.

In recent years, however, many churches had an implosion due to a shortage of caregivers. That shortage was partially due to the lack of expectations for group leaders to enlist a team. Because leaders and caregivers were undiscovered and undeveloped, they were unequipped as disciples and were not ready for other church roles. Since there was no other leadership development pipeline in these churches, the impact was painful.

WHEN OUR LEADERS ARE CARING, THEY IMPACT BUSINESSES, SCHOOLS, AND THE MARKETPLACE.

There are many shortages in younger-age groups (especially preschool and children) in churches today. Without new leaders, new groups cannot start. Without prepared leaders, some ministries cannot continue.

In addition, the span of care for groups also impacts the church. If groups are understaffed, then care suffers not only in the group but also in the church. When leaders and care are in short supply throughout the church, people disconnect. As a result, attendance declines as care is reduced and needs go unmet.

THE WORLD

I want you to think about the impact of group leaders and care team members upon the world. When our leaders are caring, they impact businesses, schools, and the marketplace. When Christian leaders discover and develop their abilities in the safe environment of the group, they prepare to step forth into the world.

When group members and leaders see their groups organized to care, they also learn how to lead secular organizations to do so. When they see group leaders train members, they learn how to challenge and communicate with those they lead at work, school, and play.

In turn, the world sees how caring our members and leaders are to each other and to others. When we live out the love of our Savior, our care attracts them. Indeed, it is true: *"By this everyone will know that you are my disciples, if you love one another."* Our genuine care for each other results in a world that can see Jesus' love in us.

HOW TO ENLIST YOUR CARE TEAM

There was a time when an invitation to serve in a church or group was a high honor. It was acknowledgment that someone recognized potential in the individual. In fact, many were eager to serve. Mass enlistment efforts often produced plentiful results.

Those days are over. People are busy, often too busy. Pulpit announcements of leadership needs seldom produce worthwhile results. Life today has trained people to say no.

Because of the leadership shortage, good enlistment steps often break down. Prayer is often quick or missing. Pressure to fill an empty position too often leads to acceptance of warm bodies rather than God-called individuals.

It does not have to be that way. I want to share some simple steps. Fight the pressure to rush. Follow God's leadership. Start small and do it right. Be persistent and watch what He does!

STEP 1: PRAY AND WAIT. In Matthew 9, we read about Jesus doing ministry in all the towns and villages. In response to what He was seeing, we read: *When he saw the crowds, he felt compassion for them, because they were distressed and dejected, like sheep without a shepherd. Then he said to his disciples, "The harvest is abundant, but the workers are few. Therefore, pray* *to the Lord of the harvest to send out workers into his harvest"* (Matthew 9:36-38).

Notice, Jesus did not command the disciples (and us) to bring all the potential leaders to Him. He did not say, Do a survey to discover spiritual gifts. No, he said to pray to the Lord of the harvest, and He would be the one who would send the workers we need.

Plain and simple, your job is to pray for workers. Have you prayed? Are you praying, believing He will answer your prayer? Or are you trying to do His work for Him? Pray, believe He will send them, and then watch to see Him at work.

The "fixer" in me wants to provide quick solutions to problems. But I have learned to be patient as I wait for His timing. I have learned to pray realizing that this is God's work, and He always knows more than I do. Sometimes we need to learn patience. And so, we wait for God to send the worker(s) we need.

The season of prayer may be long or short. At times, I have prayed and immediately God provided the answer for my enlistment need. Let me be clear: in my experience quick answers tend to be uncommon. But the right leader is always worth the wait. So be patient as you pray for the workers He will send.

STEP 2: WATCH. While you are praying, look around in the group and beyond the group. Is God at work in someone? Did He bring someone to you or to your awareness? Did another leader talk to you about someone? Without sharing the focus of your prayer, did an individual share what God has laid on his or her heart? Watch. Listen.

As you watch, take your observations to the Lord in prayer. Allow Him to lead. Don't get ahead of Him. Remember, the disciples Jesus called did not look like world changers, but they were! Watch where God is at work in individuals and join God there.

STEP 3: ASK, "WILL YOU HELP ME?" Continue to pray. Don't ask the individual to fill a role or position. Instead, ask the individual that God has laid on your heart to help you with a small task. Observe him or her as you do ministry and life together. Continue to invite the person to assist you with tasks related to the role for which you asked God

WATCH WHERE GOD IS AT WORK IN INDIVIDUALS AND JOIN GOD THERE.

for workers. Continue giving the potential leader experiences. Write down some of your observations.

STEP 4: INVITE TO SERVE. When you are sure that the individual is the one God sent for the role, make an appointment for a face-to-face conversation. This should not be a short, hallway conversation.

After thanking him for taking time to talk with you, tell him that you prayed (step 1) that God would send someone to serve in the role you sought to fill. Tell him that God laid him on your heart, and as a result you watched what God was doing in his life (step 2). Share some of the things you observed. Then share that because of the prayer and observation, you invited him to join you in doing ministry and life together (step 3). Share some of the observations you made from those interactions. Explain to him that prayer and observation led you to conclude (step 4) that he will serve well in the role for which you asked God to send a leader. Tell him how you have seen him grow in competence and confidence as you served together.

Then, ask him to pray for a week before giving you an answer. Check back in a week. If the answer is yes, thank him and continue to support, coach, and pray for him. Share the good news with the group and ask for their prayers and support.

If the answer is no, express your disappointment without producing guilt. Ask if there is another place of service for which he believes God may be preparing him. Pledge your continued prayers. Accept the answer and begin the four steps again.

In my experience, after prayer and observation you will be more likely to find the worker God sends. If you allow time for prayer and observation, I believe God will help you make good assessments about whether the worker is the one. And your observations will become evidence that will give the individual confidence that he or she has the competence to fill the role well. I believe fewer will say no to God and to you about serving when you take these four enlistment steps.

ENLISTING CARE TEAM MEMBERS FROM BOTH GENDERS

In men's and boys' groups, when we seek care team members, we enlist males. In women's and girls' groups, we enlist females. But what about in coed groups?

In my experience, the more caring of the two genders is female. So, when we enlist caregivers to lead a coed group to provide care, we tend to ask females first. Here are some reasons why this is *not* ideal:

1. Coed groups often have a mix of married and unmarried individuals.

2. Some spouses of males in coed groups serve in younger-age groups, meaning the husband is the only one in the group.

3. We want to avoid asking people of the opposite gender to visit, call, text, or email with one another.

4. When female care team members communicate with a married couple, they tend to connect with females.

5. Males on average have fewer friends and are more likely to drop out than females. That means that males need contact even more than females.

What can we do about this situation in coed groups? I suggest enlisting both male and female care team members. A simple solution is to organize and communicate with subgroups by gender. This strengthens male interactions and relationships. Single-gender subgroups (or care groups) may also be useful during teaching time depending on the lesson.

In some cases, enlisting male care team members may take even more time. But our groups and our churches need *more* males rather than *fewer*. Pray and follow the four steps outlined and help them understand the need for males. Patient enlistment of your care team will be worth every minute eventually. The results will be worth the time! Gather God-called care team members who will join you in saying, "We care!"

SECTION TWO: ORGANIZING FOR CARE

REFLECTION QUESTIONS

1. CHAPTER 4: What is the role of the group's teacher or leader and apprentice related to the care team?

2. CHAPTER 4: Which member of the care team is most needed right now by your group? Why?

3. CHAPTER 4: Why are Greeters and Hosts (see Appendices 3A and 3B) an important part of the care team?

4. CHAPTER 5: In the chapter subsection "The Church," I mention a shortage of leaders. How can enlisting a care team help the church address this shortage?

5. CHAPTER 5: Which of the four enlistment steps do you believe has been skipped or neglected most often? Why?

6. CHAPTER 5: What are the benefits of asking, "Will you help me?"

SECTION THREE: COMMUNICATING CARE

Mike met Buster in the church hallway a few minutes before their separate meetings. Mike stopped Buster and said, "You were right. Adding a care team has really helped. I am convinced that the additional care has strengthened relationships and led to our group averaging twelve attenders for the last month."

Mike added, "I believe the group is ready to help with the care. How do I lead them that way?"

Buster smiled and said, "Mike, I agree. They're ready. Your next steps are to share your group's contact information with group members, teach them about meaningful conversation, and then ask your care team to begin assigning absentee and friend care contacts."

Mike asked, "How will sharing contact information help?"

Buster replied, "How can group members help care if they don't have access to contact information of members and friends?"

Mike replied, "Makes a lot of sense. What do you mean by 'meaningful conversation'?"

Buster replied, "There are three levels of communication: habit, weather, and meaningful. *Meaningful* has the most opportunity for care. We will talk more about that after our meetings."

CHAPTER 6

GATHERING CONTACT INFORMATION

Imagine discovering that a member of your group lost his mother. You pick up the phone to call him and discover the number you have no longer works. You call the church office and discover the ministry assistant has the same invalid number. You decide to drive by his home only to discover he moved – a month ago. Now what?

Making caring contact with members, absentees, or friends is impossible without correct information. Gathering contact information and keeping it updated is essential. Sharing it with group members is vital to the life and ministry of the group.

SURVEY: How well does your group pursue and care for absentees and dropouts? (1 star = poor; 10 stars = great)

5.99
Average Rating

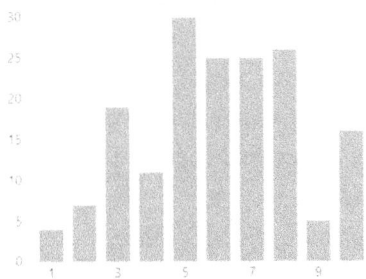

Absentees make a choice: to come or not to come. But members also have a choice: to care or not to care. When we wait to care, it becomes more embarrassing and harder for absentees to return.

In my years of experience, I have witnessed many groups with no list of members (group roll) who keep no contact information (address, phone, email, etc.). During group time in these groups, the secretary (if there is one) records an attendance number without noting who is present or absent.

This situation makes care challenging. There are at least three issues:

1. Without access to updated contact information, care may not arrive in time or may not even be possible.

2. Without good attendance records, groups tend to practice the saying, "Out of sight, out of mind." If someone is absent long enough, the group tends to forget about the person.

3. When we withhold contact information, only the pastor, group leader, or best friend may be able to provide care in time of need. This can create a bottleneck in discovering needs and expressing care. Josh Hunt in *You Can Double Your Class in Two Years or Less* says, "People who miss and are not missed, miss" (p. 99).

In a smaller group, the group leader may be able to provide all the care needed – though he or she should still share the opportunity. But when the number grows to more than five, the leader needs help in providing care. Share contact information and strengthen relationships. Raise the expectation for members to participate in making caring contacts with members, absentees, and friends. Doing so increases group involvement and connections.

Share friends' contact information with the group. What

David Francis says about new members in *Invite I-6: A Six-Lane Strategy Toward an Inviting Sunday School* could also apply to friends: "Help new members of your group identify those . . . the class could help them reach" (p. 43).

USE IT OR LOSE IT

Updated contact information is essential for care. One of the best ways to keep contact information up-to-date is to use it often. For instance, *UPDATED CONTACT INFORMATION* attenders in the group I attend write *IS ESSENTIAL FOR CARE.* down their prayer requests. A volunteer emails the requests to members, absentees, and others on Sunday or Monday. This is a weekly test of email accuracy. If one bounces, we contact the person to get it right. If there is a need for care, we know it and provide care quickly.

The same process works for phone and text numbers. Use them often. If any fail, seek the correct number quickly. An additional method is to print, text, or email contact information for all members, asking members to look over their information and update information needing change. My group does this quarterly and discovers and makes changes each time.

SURVEY: How well does your group connect with and care for new members? (1 star = poor; 10 stars = great)

7.11
Average Rating

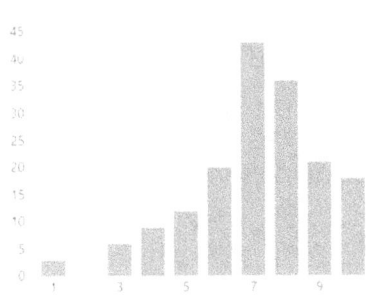

When we care well for guests, they are more likely to become new members. When we care well for new members, they are more likely to stay. What can you do to improve your care for them?

When someone joins the group, update information you already have. When guests visit, ask them to complete a registration form. Help them understand why this information is important. See chapter 18 for more information.

Add new members to your member care list and your guests to your friend care list. Your group uses these lists to pray for them, invite them to group events, and reach out in times of need. Many guests will agree to become part of your care list when you describe it that way, communicating, "We care!"

SURVEY: How well does your group connect with, care for, and invite people from the community? (1 star = poor; 10 stars = great)

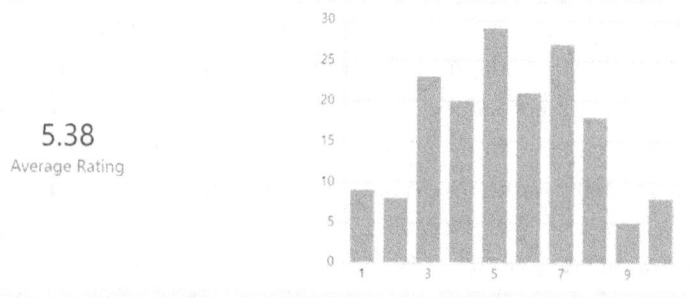

5.38
Average Rating

Reflect on the survey scores of the three graphs in this chapter. Notice that the scores are best for caring for new members, next for absentees, and worst for friends (people in the community). How can we raise our care for all three this year? Let's neglect none of the three!

CHAPTER 7

LEVELS OF COMMUNICATION

Most relationships do not stay healthy without regular inter-action and communication. However, even regular doses of communication can produce shallow relationships. The same is true for relationships with group members and friends.

THREE COMMUNICATION CATEGORIES

I tend to oversimplify communication into three categories: habit, weather, and meaningful. *Habit* is superficial commu-nication that requires no thought. It is often simply a reflex, like responding to someone who says hello. *Weather* is com-municating about issues that reveal little about the individual or his or her feelings, like talking about what happened at the ball game. *Meaningful* is communication revealing self, along with thoughts, struggles, questions, emotions, etc.

There is little depth or trust necessary for habit communica-tion. But we move a little deeper for weather communication. We believe the other person will humor our conversation due to relationship or role. But we build meaningful conversation on time, trust, and care. We care about the conversation because we care about the person. The more we invest, the stronger the relationship.

MOVING FROM SHALLOW TO DEEPER

How do we move group members from shallow, superficial levels of communication to deeper levels? Individuals and entire groups may operate primarily on habit and weather communication. We may even treat Bible study lessons that way: as historical lectures about the Bible rather than conversations with God and each other about how we struggle to live out the truth of God's Word.

The moment we discover an affinity (something we have in common) may be when we feel comfortable moving deeper. Or needs during a crisis may open the door

THE MOMENT WE DISCOVER AN AFFINITY (SOMETHING WE HAVE IN COMMON) MAY BE WHEN WE FEEL COMFORTABLE MOVING DEEPER.

for conversation about help. What if group leaders could help members take steps from the shore into deeper waters of caring communication? Moving from no relationship to caring relationships between members and friends can happen through conversation, but relationships can also strengthen through intentionality and events.

CONVERSATIONAL CARE

My friend Ron practiced moving conversation to a more caring level a few months ago. Neither of us knew Kevin when the starter paired us with him for a round of golf. We started with habit conversation, greeting one another. Before we teed off, Ron introduced himself and asked Kevin's name. I introduced myself. We all shook hands. Names are important, but up to this point we had exchanged nothing meaningful.

We talked on the weather level for the first two holes, focused on golf. We moved into meaningful conversation when Ron asked caring questions focused on getting to know Kevin. He asked about his golf background, his family, and work. Ron listened well, and we both shared meaningful information with Kevin.

Later, Ron shared about his return to the area to be closer to family. He shared about his ministry work prior to retirement. That opened the door for Ron to ask if Kevin was part of a church. Kevin bragged on his pastor and church for a few minutes. Ron talked about visiting churches in the area and returning to the church he and his wife had been part of earlier in ministry.

With continued conversation about life and golf, Ron invited Kevin to a group that gathers for Bible study and golfs together. Ron also mentioned a golf retreat he was planning for October. Kevin, who was returning to golf after an injury, was interested in both. Ron exchanged contact information with Kevin before we shook hands and departed.

Not every conversation will have two hours like this one did, but Ron moved toward more meaningful conversation with Kevin. During golf, Ron and I also caught up on what was happening with each other and our families. Ron and I are prayer partners. Despite now living in different states, we continue to text each other prayer requests and updates.

Often when eating in a restaurant, I ask the server's name. Then when my server brings my meal, I tell my server that I plan to pray over my food, and I ask how I may pray for him or her. Servers often greatly appreciate this move toward meaningful conversation.

CARING CONVERSATIONAL EXERCISE

Most groups have one or more extroverts, but not all extroverts know how to move conversation toward care. What if you gathered your group for a few minutes during a group Bible study session (or a group event: social, project, or meal) to practice moving conversation toward deeper levels of care?

Consider these ideas for a fifteen-minute practice session:

1. Divide the group into pairs (use same-gender pairs in coed groups)

2. In two to three minutes, explain the three levels of conversation: habit, weather, and meaningful.

3. Practice habit conversation in pairs. Then ask the group what action to take to make habit conversation more caring. Have pairs practice adding care to habit conversation.

4. Practice weather conversation (talk about the weather this time) in pairs. Then ask pairs to talk about how to make weather conversation more caring. Have pairs practice adding care to weather conversation.

5. Ask pairs to practice meaningful conversation (share a brief concern about work, family, or a prayer request). Have pairs add care to the meaningful conversation and pray together.

6. Debrief as a group.

7. Make an assignment: ask group members to add care to conversations this week and come prepared to share about their efforts (successful or not).

8. Remind them during the week. And next time you are together, call for reports.

What results would you expect from your group? Even in the most caring group, this exercise can raise caring conversation beyond habit. If we move toward more caring and meaningful conversation with the group, those experiences will prepare us to be more caring with family, friends, and those in our community. Caring conversation is an essential part of expressing, "I care!" I will share additional avenues for expressing care toward members, absentees, and friends in the chapters ahead.

CHAPTER 8

COMMUNICATING CARE WITH MEMBERS AND FRIENDS

The group's leader and members of the group's care team cannot do this work alone. A key phrase on many of the job descriptions for care team members in Appendices 3A and 3B is "Lead the group to . . . ." The job of care team members is not to do the work for the group. The job is to mobilize the entire group to carry out this important work of care.

Why? Two important reasons are that our Lord commanded us to love one another and to make disciples of all nations. In fact, leading the group to love God, care for one another and others, and make disciples are core purposes of what our groups do. What would happen if we treated our friends as if they were group members (like the testimony below)?

> **TESTIMONY:** WE TRY TO KEEP THESE FRIEND-
> SHIPS CLOSE TO MEMBERS OF THE GROUP; WE
> TRY TO TREAT THEM LIKE GROUP MEMBERS.

There are several key times for communicating related to caring for members, absentees, and friends. Consider the following moments for care:

BEFORE THE SESSION

Some communication needs to be shared one-on-one. Did Billy make the absentee contact you assigned? If not, asking him in front of the group may create guilt and embarrassment. If he did talk with the absentee, the group may need to know what he discovered, unless it was confidential.

When care team members listen well before the session, they may share prayer requests discovered in conversations. When event plans need help, this time gives opportunity to accept or confirm assignments before announcements during the session. Take the time to listen face-to-face with care before the session.

DURING THE SESSION

The start of the group session is the ideal time to make announcements that everyone needs to hear. Avoid announcements intended for one person. Share details about upcoming socials, projects, or meals. Discuss ministry plans that need group participation. Have a season of prayer for member and friend needs, group plans, and goals.

GROUP TIME

Set aside 20 percent of your group time for your care team to lead in the important work of care. Focus on absentees and friends who need contact and care. Greet each other. Welcome and register guests. Ask for reports of care for members and friends. Notice those who are absent and make assignments to reach out in care (for example, send a text or email during care team time). Make assignments to reach out to and care for friends. Ask for prayer requests and pray together. The teacher or leader may also use subgroups to help with part of the lesson. These assignments may lead to additional affinity discovery and relationship development.

AFTER THE SESSION

Much care will take place after group time. If your group meets on Sunday morning, visit with guests and walk them to their children, restrooms, and worship. Follow up on a prayer request and pray with individuals. Make contact assignments. Ask care team members if they need help with socials, projects, or meal plans. Visit with members and get to know them better. Send a quick text to someone you missed.

BETWEEN SESSIONS

There are 166-167 hours between group times. Use them for care. Gather to make event plans. Enjoy a fellowship together. Eat a meal together as a group, care team, or with a member or friends. Serve together in a church or community project. Make caring contacts by mail, phone, email, text, or a visit (face-to-face). Respond to discovered needs.

> **TESTIMONY:** A LADY RECENTLY RETURNED FOR THE FIRST TIME SINCE THE PANDEMIC. SHE TOLD OUR GROUP THAT OVER THE YEARS SHE HAD RECEIVED NOTES OF ENCOURAGEMENT ALWAYS ARRIVING JUST WHEN SHE NEEDED THEM MOST.

CARE TEAM COMMUNICATION METHODS

Care team members will want to set up quick and easy methods of communicating with each other and the group. You may set up a group for your care team, a portion of the team, or for the entire group. There are many options available today. Consider the following:

- SOCIAL MEDIA CLOSED GROUPS. If you choose this option, I suggest choosing an option that allows a closed group (meaning no one from outside the group can view the members or anything posted). A closed group requires approval before adding anyone new to the group. This ensures confidentiality and safety. For instance, if the group is open, sharing a prayer request about a group member on vacation or at the funeral home can alert thieves.

- DIGITAL GROUPS. This can be email, text, Zoom, or another web-based app. Teach group members to avoid posting individual messages in the digital group – only post information needed by the entire group. This makes reading posts more manageable.

- PHONE GROUP. This can be a mass call, a phone chain or tree, or another app service (CallingPost currently is free for groups of up to ten people, with some limitations). Write out, rehearse, and keep your voice messages brief. Read the message to someone first to make sure all the information needed is in the message. Everyone prefers one complete message to a partial message followed by a correction.

TESTIMONY: EACH WEEK I SEND AT LEAST ONE CARD AND ONE TEXT AND MAKE ONE PHONE CALL TO SOMEONE. I FOCUS ON SENIORS OR THOSE I KNOW WHO ARE STRUGGLING.

Be wise in your expressions of care. Care should be timely, appropriate, and appreciated. Without thinking, we may violate these requirements. Allow me to illustrate.

Asking a lady who miscarried the previous week when she is due (or one who is not pregnant) can produce great pain. I once walked up to an elderly lady before worship and greeted her with a pat on the shoulder. She nearly crawled under the pew. She had had shoulder surgery that week. Culture and background may mean that for some, hugs are not comfortable. Be sensitive in all your expressions of care. Remember that waiting two weeks to reach out with care may feel like no care at all.

SURVEY: Here are responses from 168 people to Question 5: How does your group communicate the needs of group members to the group? (Choose all that apply.)

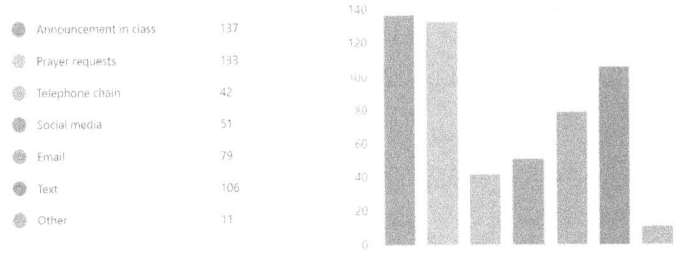

Announcement in class	137
Prayer requests	133
Telephone chain	42
Social media	51
Email	79
Text	106
Other	11

What do you see? The two highest communication methods (announcement in class and prayer requests) tend to happen during group time. The next two highest (text and email) are more likely to occur between group sessions.

SECTION THREE: COMMUNICATING CARE

REFLECTION QUESTIONS

1. CHAPTER 6: Why is it important to share contact information with group members?

2. CHAPTER 6: How does "use it or lose it" relate to contact information? Since regular attenders may not require contact as often, how do we keep their records updated?

3. CHAPTER 7: What are the three levels of communication? Which level do your members use most before Bible study begins?

4. CHAPTER 7: How might the Caring Conversational Exercise help your group?

5. CHAPTER 8: Taking advantage of which of the moments for care (Before the Session, During the Session, etc.) has the greatest potential for helping your group? Why?

6. CHAPTER 8: Which of the three communication methods shared would work best for your care team? Why?

SECTION FOUR:
TRUST, RELATIONSHIPS, AND EVENTS

Buster ran into Mike making copies in the church office. Buster asked, "How are you? And how is your group doing?"

Mike replied, "I'm doing well, but I am starting to worry about the group. Attendance has dipped this summer, and it's hard to get anyone to come to our events."

Buster asked, "How well does the group know each other? Do they trust each other? If they needed help, would they ask group members?"

Mike answered, "They know names, but I am not sure about trust. What does that have to do with attendance?"

Buster said, "Trust leads to honesty and transparency with the group. Trust enables members to share life and spiritual struggles and ask for help."

Buster added, "A healthy balance of socials, projects, and meals can help build trust between sessions. People want to be around those they can trust."

Mike asked, "We have had parties and meals, but what are projects, and what is the right balance for the three?"

Buster replied, "Projects strengthen relationships, reconnect absentees, and connect new friends as you work or serve together. I recommend one social, one project, and one meal each quarter."

Mike said, "Serving together might connect with some of our members. I will ask the care team to adjust our event plans."

CHAPTER 9

BUILDING TRUST

Of the many values of caring relationships, trust is one of the most important. When we trust the people in a group, we choose to invest time, energy, and conversation with the group. In fact, when trust is high, there is often a desire to increase time with the group. In time of need, there is no hesitation to ask for help, and when it is possible, there is no hesitation from group members to meet needs.

In some groups, relationships are friendly but are not built on trust. Knowledge about group members and conversations is superficial (see chapter 8). Spontaneous or planned interactions seldom occur between group times. Lessons often focus on history and biblical facts rather than application of the truth. Personal needs go unshared. Even prayer requests are often about others. Guests are not frequent and seldom return.

Without trust, investment of time and energy into the relationship slows or ceases. Without intervention, engagement in lessons, conversation, and group time becomes less important and relationships drift apart. Strong relationships and trust enable the group to work through conflict and challenging times. Caring leadership matters. May we never hear our Lord say, *"Woe to the shepherds who destroy and scatter the sheep of my pasture!"* (Jeremiah 23:1).

What can we do to lead group members to lean into trust and caring relationships? What steps can leaders and care team members take to increase trust? Consider the following ideas:

1. HONESTY AND TRANSPARENCY. Teaching and communication are key areas where practicing honesty and transparency can impact trust. When group members feel comfortable enough to share their thoughts, feelings, and struggles, then trust is healthy. On a recent Sunday, the group in which I participate had two newer group members in tears as they revealed spiritual struggles during bouts with cancer. The group responded with listening, care, and support. This interaction came after the group's leader (Mike) over several weeks asked members to write and share salvation testimonies. Over the years, Mike has been transparent in his teaching, sharing about the impact of his biological family, struggles with a neighbor, and more. Example and leadership matter. Mike's example increased trust and prepared group members to take risks in honest sharing.

2. DEPENDABILITY AND CONSISTENCY. When a member promises to help in time of need but does not show up, that causes trust to diminish. Keeping promises matters. Timeliness of response to crisis also matters. When we wait too long to help, the need may pass, and trust may decline. To rebuild trust requires dependability and consistency (dependability over time). Keeping commitments matters.

3. LISTENING. Listening to understand is essential. Too often we listen in order to respond, and we miss what the other person said. Listening is a gift. It helps when listeners practice patience and ask caring questions. When we

do so consistently, the one speaking feels care, and trust grows. Care team members bless group members when they receive training and then share training sessions about active listening.

4. KINDNESS AND SUPPORT. Responses to actions and conversation increase or decrease trust. The attitude and expression of our responses may communicate more than our words alone. Responses filled with anger and blame may lead to care and trust slipping away. When the response is disappointment laced with understanding, care, and prayer, then trust may grow. This is important for members of the care team to learn and communicate with the group.

There are many opportunities in group life to express care and strengthen trust. Some will be spontaneous interactions. Others will be events scheduled beyond the group Bible study session. Chapter 10 will share opportunities during teaching time to facilitate trust development. May every word and action communicate, "We care!"

CHAPTER 10

THE IMPACT OF RELATIONSHIPS AND TRUST ON TEACHING

When trust is present in groups, members desire to spend time with each other. Conversation is without fear of criticism or guilt. Members value each other. They listen well to each other, and they are unafraid to ask for prayer and help.

The presence or absence of trust among group members impacts how we teach Bible study lessons. When a group has just begun, trust needs time to develop. In big and small ways, trust is tested. Little transparency is present. Conversations and participation in the lesson are shallow. Baby steps are necessary.

After a few weeks, trust may have taken steps forward, and then a new person joins the group. The new person does not know or trust the group, and the group does not know or trust the new member. Handled well, within a few weeks the newest member may have learned to trust the leader and group. But if another new member joins, the cycle begins again.

An additional challenge arises when new members join over several months, causing a constant ebb and flow of trust. Without good leadership and care, groups give up and settle for not knowing or trusting each other. Conversations and lessons are shallow. Honesty and openness are rare. Transparency is missing.

This can also happen in groups that have been together for a long time. Members are busy. They go through the motions. They give up on investing in knowing one another. Trust becomes superficial based upon previous levels of relationship development. In the same way in which we need an ongoing, fresh relationship with God, we need fresh, trusting relationships with group members.

The group mission and discipleship are at stake. When a group lacks trust, the teacher or leader tends to prepare and teach generic lessons without specific application to group members and their needs. The questions demand no risk by group members who give "weather" answers rather than "meaningful" ones (see chapter 7 about the two terms). Everyone hesitates to share feelings, struggles, or needs. Despite efforts by the leader, the lesson stays on a superficial level. Lives remain unchanged. As a result, the group abandons the mission to impact the world.

RAISING RELATIONSHIP AND TRUST LEVELS THROUGH TEACHING

A leader can influence relationships and trust-development with the group, but if no one initiates movement, then poor habits develop. It is important for the leader to spend time talking with and getting to know group members before and after Bible study group time. If group members know and trust the leader, they will be more willing to follow and take risks.

In addition, in the early weeks it is helpful to lead the new group to talk with each other. To avoid the fear of public speaking, the teacher or leader makes assignments in groups of two to five people. Talking in groups of this size feels more like conversation rather than public speaking. In newer groups, sharing brief introductions and answers to questions can help members take beginning steps toward getting to know one another and toward trust.

Interaction and conversation are essential. If the teacher or leader does all the talking, the only relationship and trust that will grow is with the leader. That means the leader desiring to increase trust and develop relationships will limit himself or herself to talking less than 50 percent of group time. Working in smaller groups for a few minutes is one solution to enable more members to talk.

Another way the teacher or leader can enable the group to take relational and trust risks is through self-disclosure and being transparent. When group members realize that they are not the only ones who fail and struggle, they identify with the leader and feel more comfortable sharing. In most cases, the leader's example results in greater relational and trust growth.

Asking thought-provoking questions will also increase responses. But how do we get more group members to respond? Groups have inner and outer thinkers. Outer thinkers tend to think out loud. Inner thinkers need time to process before responding. When the teacher or leader asks a question, outer thinkers tend to respond first. One approach to involve inner thinkers is for the leader to call *INTERACTION AND CONVERSATION ARE ESSENTIAL.* for reflection for thirty seconds before asking for answers from those who have not previously responded.

It is important for the leader to affirm responses. If the response is off-the-wall or wrong, criticizing may shut down future responses by that individual and by the group. Instead, ask how the person came to that conclusion. At times, it may be necessary to disagree in a kind way. Or it may be necessary to thank the person and move on by asking if there are other thoughts.

The way the leader and group respond in times like these can have a dramatic impact on group relationships and trust.

If the leader or a member overreacts in one session, an apology to the individual privately as well as in front of the group can go a long way toward restoring trust. Dealing with issues privately helps limit embarrassment and maintain higher levels of trust. The public apology raises the value of relationships in front of the whole group. May every lesson build trust that communicates, "We care!"

CIRCLES AND SEMICIRCLES

Conversation, trust, and care tend to flourish in an environment where everyone can see one another. Since a sizable portion of communication is visual (facial expressions and gestures), I encourage groups to use circles and semicircles. These seating arrangements allow attenders to see, hear, and understand each other better. Every space with chairs can accommodate as many people in circles or semicircles as in rows. I have tested it and it works well.

GROUP COVENANTS

I want to share one final thought on raising trust through teaching. Sometimes it helps to have a verbal or written group-member covenant about how to respond and relate in group sessions and in relationships with each other. Covenants may address faithfulness, participation, confidentiality, no judgment, prayer for each other, etc. Keeping our covenant agreements builds trust. When someone pushes the established boundaries, we gently remind them about the covenant. Even these reminders build trust.

CHAPTER II

GROUP EVENTS: SOCIALS, PROJECTS, AND MEALS

Each week, there are 166-167 hours beyond the group session. That means much time is available to invest in relationships and increase trust. We all need people who care for us. Gathering for events allows time to talk, get to know each other, and discover things in common with friends who become like family. We connect beyond the superficial ways we may know one another from our Bible study sessions.

Events are not just for members. Groups benefit from inviting absentees and friends to group events. These socials, projects, and meals enable members to spend time with absentees and new friends. There they meet one another, discover affinities, and have fun. The result is often deeper relationships and the desire to spend time together beyond group sessions and planned events.

There are three major benefits of group events. Consider the following:

- RELATIONSHIPS. As groups get to know and trust each other, teaching and learning can become more applicable. Positive accountability (encouragement) increases. The group leader prepares lessons and applies the truth to real-life situations. Events – whether socials, projects, or meals – strengthen relationships in ways that group time is unable to do alone. People discover affinities as they eat, talk, laugh, and work with others. They connect and bond. We share the love of our ultimate relationship with Jesus as we care.

- ASSIMILATION. Without friendships, people often drop out. Events are natural opportunities for members to reconnect with absentees and dropouts. Care team members encourage the group to invite everyone on the care list every time they plan an event. Those who have missed Bible study sessions can re-engage in relationships away from group time and feel more comfortable easing back into attendance because of these events together.

- REACHING. While events help us reconnect absentees, they can also help us introduce new people to the group. When friends attend our events, they get to know and discover affinities with group members. This enables guests to be more open to an invitation to attend a Bible study group session. Events are great tools to help us reach out with care to show the love of Christ. Jesus dined with sinners. Let's invite new people and those who don't yet know Jesus to our events, with the goal of getting to know them and leading them to Christ.

Josh Hunt, author of *You Can Double Your Class in Two Years or Less,* encourages inviting "every member and every prospect to every fellowship every month." I support the intentionality for groups to plan events monthly. My suggestion is to plan one of each type of event every quarter: social, project, and meal.

> **TESTIMONY:** WE ARE A YOUNG-ADULT GROUP, SO BABY SHOW-
> ERS, WEDDING SHOWERS, AND SOCIAL EVENTS ARE OUR FOCUS.

Allow me to stereotype a little. On average, women are more social than men. And men often prefer to develop relationships while working on a project together. Yes, some men love social events, and some women prefer projects. And everyone likes to eat. Providing one of each type of event every quarter means that plans will often connect with each member, absentee, and friend at least two out of three times that we plan events.

Consider these three broad categories of group events: socials, projects, and meals. They are not meant to be exclusive. But these categories should provide plenty of reminders and ideas that can be useful in other kinds of events.

SURVEY: What are ways your group has strengthened relationships and provided care for group members in the last three years? (Choose all that apply.)

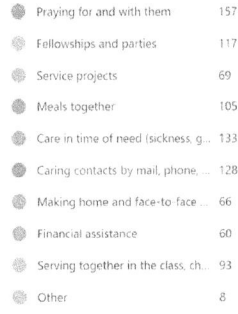
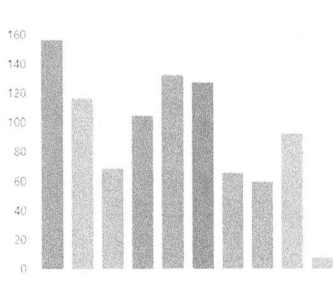

Praying for and with them	157
Fellowships and parties	117
Service projects	69
Meals together	105
Care in time of need (sickness, g...	133
Caring contacts by mail, phone, ...	128
Making home and face-to-face ...	66
Financial assistance	60
Serving together in the class, ch...	93
Other	8

What do you see in this graph? How important are events (socials, projects, and meals) to relationships and care?

SOCIAL EVENTS: FELLOWSHIPS AND PARTIES

Social events focus on relationships, conversation, and fun. They may or may not include food or a meal. They may be at church, in a home, or at another location. While the audience may vary, we plan most social events for a mix of group members, absentees, and friends.

There are hundreds of social-event possibilities: a bonfire, hayride, game night, bowling, skeet shooting, quilting bee, attending a ball game, playing softball, skating, skiing, fishing, riding bikes, camping, birthday celebrations, Christmas or holiday party, tailgate party, book club, and lots more. Two people or many can enjoy these social events. They may even be spontaneous.

Some social events may need to be tweaked to increase the value for developing caring relationships. For instance, watching a movie together or attending a Christian concert may have little value (for developing caring relationships) unless you connect it to some questions for conversation or a meal before or after the movie or concert. When making social plans, keep the purposes in mind: strengthen relationships, reconnect absentees, and connect with new friends through relationships, conversation, and fun.

PROJECTS: WORKING OR SERVING TOGETHER

The point of projects is to strengthen relationships, reconnect absentees, and connect with new friends as you work or serve together or help a person or organization in need. A social event can become a project when it adds an element of working or serving. An example might be if your skating event becomes a fundraiser for a homeless shelter.

As your group carries out the Great Commission to make disciples of all nations, connecting with people in the community and the world is important. If invited, some friends outside the group will join us for projects. Some enjoy working, serving, and/or helping others. Don't say no for them. Ask them!

> **TESTIMONY:** WE DID YARD CLEANUP IN THE CITY PARK WITH THE GROUP. A MEAL PRECEDES EVERY GATHERING.

Of the hundreds of project opportunities for working, serving, and helping others, here are a few: an after-school tutoring program, childcare for parents' night out, single moms' oil change, VBS (Vacation Bible School) for daycare children, building a handicap ramp, simple home repairs for senior adults, building a Habitat for Humanity home, painting a pregnancy support center building, appreciation meal for elementary school teachers or firemen, family support following a fire, and so many more.

A few years ago, my church announced plans for a church workday to update the landscaping prior to Easter. A member of the senior men's group invited his unchurched neighbor who had a beautiful lawn. *DON'T SAY NO FOR THEM. ASK THEM!* He came with his tools and got to know group members as they worked, talked, and laughed together that day. He enjoyed his time with the group so much that he showed up for Bible study the next day. It was his first time in a church. On the sixth week of attending, he professed faith in Jesus. A good relationship with a neighbor plus an invitation to a work project resulted in Bible study group and worship attendance as well as salvation and discipleship.

MEALS: EATING TOGETHER

Everyone must eat. They can be meals together as a group or one-on-one. They can be spontaneous or planned and announced. Meals can be in homes, restaurants, or church. Eating together is often relaxing, while enabling conversational discovery. Meals may accompany socials or projects, or they may focus on eating and conversation. What if you took a few minutes during the meal for those at the same table to share some fun facts about themselves?

Many Bible study groups meeting in homes eat together weekly. But keep in mind that eating together at other times can be helpful for groups and members to connect with friends and reconnect with absentees. Raise the value of eating together. Challenge group members to invite absentees and friends for meals at restaurants or at home. Get acquainted. Listen. Care. Since they are going to eat anyway, it won't cost much extra time, and the money spent on the meal will be a kingdom investment.

Like socials and projects, there are many special options for eating together from which groups may choose. Consider some of the following: a women's tea; picnic; eating out; meal after worship; breakfast at church before group time; meal during group time; special holiday meal; progressive dinner (appetizers or salad at the first house, main course at the second house, and dessert at the third house); potluck; dessert fellowship; brown food; donuts; pizza; fruit-and-veggie trays; and so much more.

PLAN SOME MEALS, AND WATCH CONNECTIONS AND DISCIPLESHIP GROW.

Meals are so versatile. Add decorations and make a meal special. Add something fun to the meal experience and turn it into a social. Add work or fundraising to a meal and make it a project. Eat together for teacher or leader appreciation and make it a social. Again, don't forget to include absentees and friends in your meal plans and invitations.

I want to share one more thought about meals. Meals tend to require less time than socials or projects. That makes them more appealing to some members, absentees, and guests. And, as I said, we must eat anyway. Plan some meals, and watch connections and discipleship grow.

SPONTANEOUS EVENTS

Socials, projects, and meals can be events planned by care team members for the entire group or a portion of the group. But group members with no formal plan can enjoy them as well. In other words, two friends or couples can go bowling or to a ball game. They can grill out or help a neighbor with a handicap ramp. Simply stated, spontaneous events are people doing life together.

SURVEY: What are ways in the last three years that your group has developed relationships and provided care for people in the community who are not members of your class or church? (Choose all that apply.)

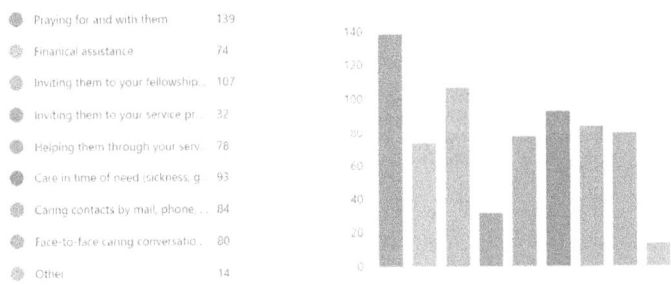

Prayer and socials are first and second for relationships and care for friends. What does your group do with friends?

We can also plan spontaneous events. I know, that sounds like an oxymoron – but here are a couple of ideas. Ask group members to plan a social, project, or meal with a friend. Or challenge group members to plan four-by-four fellowships designed for *four* people (or couples) to take turns making social, meal, or project plans each month for *four* months. Challenge them to invite friends to be one or two of the four.

With planned spontaneous events, give a deadline to arrange and conduct these events. This idea works even better if the leader extending the challenge announces what he has planned and who he has invited. You will be hearing reports from these spontaneous events for weeks!

INVITE IN-SERVICE MEMBERS

I encourage you to include in-service members in your events. These are members who left your group to teach in younger age groups (preschool, children, or teens) or are serving in some other capacity. Invite them. By including them, you continue to strengthen your connections with them. And you may prevent leaders in younger age groups from burning out from lack of time and relationships with adults.

> **TESTIMONY:** OUR GROUP HAS SOME COUPLES SERVING AS ASSISTANTS IN OTHER GROUPS WHO CAN'T JOIN US ON SUNDAY MORNING. WE KNOW THEY STILL NEED TO BE CARED FOR AS WELL. WE INTENTIONALLY SEEK WAYS TO INCLUDE THEM VIA FELLOWSHIP OR SERVICE EVENTS, SOCIAL MEDIA/DIGITAL, ETC.

I also encourage you to find a way to share group prayer requests with in-service members that allows them to share their prayer requests. For instance, the group I attend passes a clipboard around for members to write down prayer requests. Group members, including absentees and in-service members, receive them by email on Monday. Social media apps that allow closed groups (only approved members can see posts) also allow you to communicate with absentees and in-service members.

Which type of event is your personal favorite? Keep in mind that members and friends may have a different favorite. Expand your time together through socials, projects, and meals. Communicate "we care" by inviting absentees and friends.

SECTION FOUR: TRUST, RELATIONSHIPS, AND EVENTS

REFLECTION QUESTIONS

1. CHAPTER 9: Of the four steps shared for increasing trust, which step could benefit your group the most?

2. CHAPTER 10: What can you and your group do to increase trust when friends visit or new members join?

3. CHAPTER 10: What actions can leaders take to enable relationships and trust? Which one is most needed by your group?

4. CHAPTER 11: Of the three major benefits of events, which one (relationships, assimilation, or reaching) is most needed by your group? Why?

5. CHAPTER 11: What is the difference between socials and projects? Which of those two types of events do your members and friends prefer? Why?

6. CHAPTER 11: Which of the three types of events (socials, projects, or meals) do you plan least often? How could inviting friends and absentees to those least-planned events increase enjoyment and participation?

SECTION FIVE: PRAYER

Buster invited Mike for lunch. After ordering, Buster said, "I've heard great comments about your lessons. You have a great care team. Your group cares well for each other. Would you like to take your care to the next level?"

Mike smiled and said, "Of course. How?"

Buster replied, "With prayer. We are caring for God's sheep. The work we do is spiritual. Your next step is to gather your care team to pray about and develop a group prayer strategy. And teach your group to pray for and with each other and with friends."

Buster continued. "You can find simple instructions for a prayer strategy retreat along with group prayer exercises on the church website."

Mike said, "I will check it out after lunch. In fact, I will ask Bob, my apprentice, to read it and take the lead on it."

Buster replied, "I have watched as God led Bob to be part of your care team and then serve as your apprentice. He will lead the effort well. Let me know if either of you needs help."

Mike replied, "Will do. Thanks for all your coaching!"

Buster said, "You're welcome. Thanks for being coachable and thanks for joining me for lunch!"

CHAPTER 12

OUR MISSION DEPENDS ON PRAYER

The work we do is spiritual business. The sheep in our care are not ours, they are God's, and not all the sheep are already in the sheep pen (John 10:16). To be obedient in the stewardship of our assignment and the sheep in our care, we need a fresh relationship with our Lord. Prayer is first a relationship and second a road map to obedience. How can we follow where our Good Shepherd leads if we don't spend time in prayer? Our mission depends on prayer.

Jesus in John 15:5 was clear that we can do nothing without Him: *"I am the vine; you are the branches. The one who remains in me and I in him produces much fruit, because you can do nothing without me."*

Prayer is conversation with God: Listening to and talking with Him. It is like breathing. It is not something extra we do; we can do nothing without prayer. How can we know Him and follow where He leads, how can we care for His sheep, without breathing in Bible study and breathing out prayer?

OUR MISSION

What is the mission of our Bible study group? It is mobilizing our group to pursue the Great Commission in the spirit of the Great Commandment. God commands us as we go to make disciples of all nations, baptizing and teaching them to obey. We are to do so with a preeminent love for God that leads us to love our neighbors and ourselves.

> **TESTIMONY:** OUR GROUP IS FULL OF WISDOM, MEANING THAT THE AVERAGE MEMBER AGE IS EIGHTY-TWO, AND WE HAVE FORTY-FIVE MEMBERS. ANY TIME *ANY* MEMBER IS SICK OR NEEDS HELP OF ANY KIND, THEY ARE ALL OVER IT WITH ASSISTANCE – FIRST WITH PRAYERS AND THEN WITH ACTION.

Our mission is huge. It is beyond the ability and power of any group or church. It is only possible to carry out this God-sized mission by joining Him on the mission. That is why it is the Great "Co-mission." We are dependent on Him. We either trust Him or we don't. We either do the mission with Him or we will be unable to do it at all.

Our vision, focus, strength, and ability to carry out the mission depend on a relationship with a great God and the power of prayer. What should our group prayer focus on as we carry out the mission? There are other focuses, but consider these two:

- WORKERS. Seeing the crowds and having compassion for them, Jesus told the disciples (and us), *"The harvest is abundant, but the workers are few. Therefore, pray to the Lord of the harvest to send out workers into his harvest."* We do not have enough workers to provide the care needed for the people He wants us to reach. Our job is to pray for those workers. That means we are to understand that

(1) we are to care for more people than we have, and (2) we are to expect the workers He will send to help with that care. When He sends them, He deserves praise – not us.

- REACHING OUT WITH PRAYER AND CARE. The care team will ask group members to share about their FRANs (friends, relatives, associates, and neighbors) and what they are facing. This will remind the group to pray and care for friends. Prayer precedes and empowers every plan and effort. As the group prays for real needs, hearts for lost and unreached people will be softened, and feet will become more aligned to reach out with care.

DEVELOPING A PRAYER STRATEGY

Gather a team to pray about and develop a prayer strategy. There is nothing wrong with talking, but make sure you spend time praying at every step. Consider these actions:

- FOCUS YOUR PRAYER STRATEGY ON CARE. Lead your group to pray and take actions to express care toward God, each other, and others. Pray with each other and with friends. Celebrate answers to prayer.

- CONDUCT AN ANNUAL RETREAT. Calendar and pray for the retreat. Gather the team – away, if possible. Spend time praying, evaluating, goal setting, and planning an effective prayer strategy. Pray and plan about the group mission and for member, absentee, friend, and community needs. Set deadlines and make assignments.

- CALENDAR PRAYER STRATEGY PROGRESS CHECKUPS. Pray together. Gather monthly to report on progress of prayer plans and adjust, as necessary. Communicate about, train, and prepare for upcoming prayer plans and events. Give everyone a responsibility to increase participation.

- ESTABLISH REGULAR PRAYER TIMES FOR BIBLE STUDY GROUPS. Put it on the calendar and in the church schedule. Seek God's leadership, blessing, and help. Pray for people, groups, and plans. Pray during group sessions and between them. Pray as a group, in pairs, and alone.

- ENCOURAGE YOUR PRAYER TEAM. Between meetings, check on leaders and their progress on prayer plans. Answer questions. Affirm excellent work. Care for them. Pray together. Remember, relationship-building and accountability work best together.

PRAY FOR MORE

I believe in prayer. God loves us and desires communion and communication. Not only do I believe in prayer, but I also believe in *big* prayers. Ask for the desires of your heart. Ask out of passion for Him and His work. Pray in faith as you ask for God-sized results!

When was the last time you prayed for God-sized results for your Bible study group? When was the last time you set aside time and gathered a group together to pray for God to bless and use your group? The need is great!

Too many groups and leaders are on life support. They are barely surviving. They exist without pursuit of purpose. They gather out of habit. They survive rather than thrive. They manage rather than lead, and if something does not change soon, the end is in sight.

Prayer is *the* significant first step toward revitalization of groups and leaders. It is *the* first step toward restoration of a fresh relationship with God. And it is *the* first step toward empowering relationships with, and care for, members, absentees, and friends. With that in mind, I want to challenge you to pray for *more*.

- Pray for *more* of God's presence, leadership, and compassion.

- Pray for *more* of His blessings and help.

- Pray for *more* eyes on the whiteness of the harvest field.

- Pray for *more* workers to be sent into the harvest.

- Pray for *more* group leaders, apprentices, care team members, and others to care for *more* people.

- Pray for *more* life-changing impact of lessons.

- Pray for *more* personal time spent in prayer and Bible study.

- Pray for *more* relationships built with friends in our community and world.

- Pray for *more* caring invitations to fellowships, projects, meals, Bible study groups, worship, and Jesus.

- Pray for *more* children, teens, and adults to accept Jesus as Savior and Lord.

- Pray for *more* disciples to grow in the likeness of Jesus.

- Pray for *more* groups to be started to care for *more* people.

- Pray for *more* relationships and for *more* needs to be met for group members and friends.

- Pray for *more* community and world impact.

If we ask God for *more* leaders and *more* groups to care for *more* people, I believe we will see much of the rest of the prayer list happen. Will you pray God-sized prayers? Will you join me in praying for *more*? May our prayers communicate to God and others, "We care!"

CHAPTER 13

PRAYING FOR AND WITH MEMBERS AND FRIENDS

Many groups do a wonderful job of praying for each other. But when was the last time you and your group spent time praying for new people? Jesus came to seek and to save the lost (Luke 19:10).

As the body of Christ, those on Jesus' heart will also be on our hearts. When we pray for something, we are *for* it. Through prayer, we make ourselves open to the Lord and His leadership in our lives about the focus of our prayers.

> **SURVEY RESULTS:** IN MY RECENT SURVEY, "PRAYING FOR AND WITH THEM" WAS THE TOP WAY GROUPS HAVE (1) STRENGTH-ENED RELATIONSHIPS AND PROVIDED CARE FOR GROUP MEMBERS, AND (2) DEVELOPED RELATIONSHIPS AND PROVIDED CARE FOR PEOPLE IN THE COMMUNITY. PRAYER MAKES A DIFFERENCE!

In the Great Commission, Jesus commanded us as His disciples to make disciples of all nations as we are going through life and the marketplace. There is still much work to do. He will draw all people to Himself (John 12:32). Jesus said, *"But I have other sheep that are not from this sheep pen; I must bring them also, and they will listen to my voice. Then there will be one flock, one shepherd"* (John 10:16).

We pursue and care for lost sheep for Him. We serve as His hands and feet to protect them from wolves and to lead them to Him. Care and prayer are life-changing!

PRAYER EXERCISES

Think about the people in your group. What are some ways your group can pray for absentees and new people? Jot down some past practices or ideas in the box below before reading further.

What would happen if you led your group to do what you just did? I want to challenge you to do so. Then set aside time to lead your members to exercise their prayer muscles in one of these ways:

1. Give group members a blank business-size card (for wallet, purse, or mirror) and ask them to write the names of two absentees and two lost or unenrolled people for whom to pray.

2. Spend time during your group session praying for absentees and new people by name.

3. Place a poster in front of the group with first names and last initial of new people for whom your group will pray (mark them off when they accept Jesus or join the group).

4. Focus prayers on new people in your assigned age group or the age group that is the focus of the church at that time.

5. Share demographics about people in your area so the group can have ideas about how to pray for new people from your community.

6. Plan cottage prayer meetings (in homes) focused on absentees and new people.

7. Distribute small dots to stick on watches or cell phones to remind people to pray for absentees and new people.

8. Set a specific time each day (like noon) to pray for absentees and new people.

9. Make appointments to call prayer partners each week and pray together for absentees and new people by name as part of the call.

10. Share testimonies about gospel conversations with lost people or those not in a Bible study group.

11. Challenge the group during conversations with new people to ask if they have prayer requests, write down the request, and pray together with them. Then remember to follow up!

12. Send out weekly email (or text) prayer-focus reminders of absentees and new people to pray for and/or their needs.

If we fail to exercise our muscles, they atrophy. Too often, we underuse our prayer muscles. Which of these prayer exercises might work well in leading your group to care for absentees and people beyond the group? Enlist a prayer team to assist you with planning and leading the exercise(s). Debrief following each experience.

> **TESTIMONY:** ONE OF THE OLDER MEN IN OUR GROUP IS NOT WALKING AS WELL AS HE USED TO, SO WE PRAYED OVER HIM, AND ALL PITCHED IN AND BOUGHT HIM AN APPLE WATCH. THE WATCH HAS FALL DETECTION AND NOTIFICATION.

PRAY AS A GROUP

To get everyone involved, I recommend subgroups with no more than six people in them. One idea is to gather group members in care groups to pray during group time, at a group event, or in homes. Another idea is to gather them in pairs or triads to pray. Pray when together. Pray by Zoom or phone. Use text or email to share requests and prayers. Don't just promise to pray; do it! And don't just pray; follow up, because you care.

PRAY WITH NEW PEOPLE

We have experienced God's love and have seen His answers to our prayers. One way we can share God's love with people in the community is to care enough about them to get to know them, ask how we can pray for them, and pray *together*. Praying with care is the best thing we can do for new friends. The simple act of conversation joined together with prayer shows that you care.

We are all busy, but you can take a few minutes to ask a question that requires more than a "weather" answer. Some new friends have never heard a prayer, and others have never had anyone pray for them out loud. Did you know that there are almost limitless places, times, and ways we can pray with a new friend? Have you prayed with a friend by phone or Zoom? Have you prayed by email, text, or social media? Have you prayed with your meal server and your hair stylist? Have you prayed while driving (without closing your eyes, of course)?

Care enough to pray for friends, and take your care to the next level by praying *with* your friends. As your friendship grows, you might even ask your friends if they want to pray. This all begins because we choose to care. We decide to ask friends how we can pray for them, and we ask for permission to pray for them and their requests.

CARE ENOUGH TO PRAY FOR FRIENDS, AND TAKE YOUR CARE TO THE NEXT LEVEL BY PRAYING WITH YOUR FRIENDS.

Praying together moves us closer together to each other and to God. When possible, follow up on a prayer request. Doing so shows we care and God cares. It provides an opportunity to celebrate answers to prayer and/ or to pray further for friends along with the situation or need.

CONFIDENTIALITY

When you discover needs in your efforts to care and pray, share those needs with your care team or your group. Look for ways to provide help for your friend. If the need is larger than you can address, ask for the help of the care team, the group, or the church. From time to time, a situation or prayer request needs referral to a professional beyond the church. Keep in mind that the major need for some requests is prayer.

Be aware that one way to ruin a relationship is to share something you heard in confidence. Don't do it! The exception is if friends threaten to harm themselves or another person or abuse a minor; then by law, you must report it. But in normal circumstances, when someone shares a need in confidence, pray with and for your friend and the situation. If appropriate, follow up with care. Be sensitive. Help if you can, but be careful not to offend, disappoint, or share the confidence.

SECTION FIVE: PRAYER

REFLECTION QUESTIONS

1. CHAPTER 12: How does the mission of your group depend on prayer?

2. CHAPTER 12: When praying, on which do you and your group focus more: workers or reaching out? How can you increase prayers for both of these?

3. CHAPTER 12: How could gathering a planning team to develop a prayer strategy help your group? What is the first step you need to take to do so?

4. CHAPTER 13: Of the prayer exercises, which three of them do you believe would connect best with your group?

5. CHAPTER 13: Why is it important to honor the request for confidentiality during prayer requests?

6. CHAPTER 13: Why is praying together *with* members, absentees, and friends so important?

SECTION SIX: SERVING SOLO AND AS A GROUP

Mike ran into Buster at the Ace Hardware store. After greeting one another, Mike said, "Buster, explain more about how our Acts 1:8 emphasis on serving will help my group."

Buster said, "By now, Mike, you understand how projects connect with some people more than meals or socials. Our Acts 1:8 emphasis will help your group focus on relationships and making disciples beyond the group and church. These serving projects will also help us connect absentees and friends who want to help."

Mike asked, "How do we discover places where we can serve?"

Buster replied, "Mike, if you led your group to brainstorm ways they could serve in the city, county, or state, I imagine you would come up with more than a dozen ideas. We anticipated your question. During a portion of next week's group-leaders meeting, we will share some serving ideas and contact information for the Acts 1:8 emphasis."

Mike said, "That will be extremely helpful. I will ask my care team to join me for the meeting. I think this emphasis will be a home run with our group."

Buster said, "Imagine the stories. Imagine the growth as disciples. Imagine the new relationships and salvations that will result. Serving creates memories and bonds that last a lifetime. Thanks, Mike."

CHAPTER 14

SERVING IN THE GROUP

In chapter 11 I shared that *projects* are useful to strengthen relationships, reconnect absentees, and connect new friends as you work or serve together. In addition, in Appendices 3A and 3B I share job descriptions for members of the group's care team. Projects and serving on the care team are two ways of serving together in the group. Helping group members in time of need is an important third way.

Paul writes, *For you were called to be free, brothers and sisters; only don't use this freedom as an opportunity for the flesh, but **serve one another through love*** (Galatians 5:13, emphasis added). Key ways to express our care toward one another are (1) serving members of our group and (2) serving with our group. There are many methods for doing so.

BECAUSE YOU CARE

Serve one another because our Lord commanded you to love one another. Serve one another because you care for Him and each other. As you pray and serve together, you will get to know one another. You will discover affinities and connections.

Relationships will deepen and care will become natural as you carry out individual and group plans and ministry.

The outcome of serving is more than the results of the ministry you do. Bonds will form. Understanding and trust will grow. Because you serve each other, you care. Because you care, you serve each other. That care for each other is how *"everyone will know that you are my disciples, if you love one another."*

Serving leads members to a greater sense of satisfaction and connection. Serving-members are more likely to develop relationships and to grow as disciples. And they are less likely to drop out.

INCREASING INVOLVEMENT IN CARE

In Appendices 3A and 3B, I share job descriptions for group members to serve on the care team. In a smaller group (five or fewer), combine the duties from those job descriptions. As an example, the teacher or group leader might also serve as the Friend Leader/Shepherd. The group's apprentice might serve as Member Leader/Shepherd.

To strengthen relationships and care, it is essential for the care team to involve as many group members as possible. One method is to add team members to the care team, especially as the group grows. For instance, you might add an apprentice Member Leader/ Shepherd or Friend Leader/Shepherd. The additional interactions from a larger team will help with the span of

SERVING LEADS MEMBERS TO A GREATER SENSE OF SATISFACTION AND CONNECTION.

care and result in more communication, affinity-discovery, and care among team members and the entire group. Adding team members will also add creativity and relationships to the group's planning and serving. I shared ideas for enlisting these additional team members in chapter 5.

A second method to involve more members in serving is for the care team to be intentional in sharing the work of care with the group, including absentees. Many job descriptions in Appendices 3A and 3B begin with the phrase, "Lead the group to . . . ." Ask group members weekly to contact and care for absentees and friends.

Seek the help of group members to plan group events (socials, projects, and meals). When absent, enlist members to cover care team member duties before and during the group session. When needs are discovered, mobilize members of the group to meet the needs.

A third method is to divide the work of the group into teams. Assign members and absentees (or seek volunteers) to each of the teams. For instance, the teams might include Discover (teaching), Connect (member care), and Invite (friend care) – from *3D Sunday School* by David Francis. By asking every member (and absentee) to serve on one of the teams, you will add creativity, interactions, and relationships. You will discover gifts, affinities, passions, and skills of people not serving on the care team. And the additional communication and interaction through serving will result in even greater care.

> **TESTIMONY:** WE HAVE STRUCTURED OUR SMALL GROUPS UPON FOUR PILLARS: APPLYING GOD'S WORD, FELLOWSHIP, PRAYER/CARE, AND MISSIONS. EACH SMALL GROUP WAS ENCOURAGED TO DESIGNATE LEADERS WITHIN THE GROUP TO OVERSEE ONE OF THE FOUR PILLARS SO THAT IT DOESN'T ALL FALL UPON THE LEADER.

THE SPAN OF CARE

As you organize your group to strengthen relationships, serve, and meet needs, keep the span-of-care ratio below 1:5 (one leader for every five members, including absentees). When the span of care grows too large (leaders caring for more than five members), care tends to decrease, resulting in lower faithfulness, care, satisfaction, and attendance. Watch and address your ratio.

INTENTIONALITY FOR RELATIONSHIP-DEVELOPMENT

As your care team and group serve together, create intentional opportunities for relationship-development. Plan relationship-building into your care team planning retreat and meetings. Pray together. If you divide group work by teams, mix up the teams annually to get to know one another better. When you plan group events, pay attention to care and relationships.

Look for opportunities to serve each other. When there is a need, respond to the need. Send encouraging cards to help with grief. Visit the hospital. Rake leaves when a member is unable to do so. Care team members are in key positions to discover, plan, and communicate opportunities for caring service. Listen well. In all you do, communicate, "We care!"

CHAPTER 15

SERVING IN THE CHURCH, COMMUNITY, AND WORLD

hrist gave us gifts and leaders *to equip the saints for the work of ministry, to build up the body of Christ* (Ephesians 4:12). The Lord disbursed those gifts among the body. They are not all possessed by one person. Likewise, group members bring a unique set of relationships, experiences, abilities, personalities, and giftedness that God desires to use *to build up the body of Christ*.

That understanding flavors the relationship-development, care, and disciple-making efforts of every Bible study group. Group members will not be fulfilled until they are fulfilling that purpose. They and the body will be less complete or built up until they are serving in the ministry of the body of Christ.

SERVING IN THE BODY OF CHRIST

Without question, a portion of the ministry of the body of Christ is in the church. Some group members may be those Christ has given to be evangelists, pastors, and teachers to equip the saints. Others will join those leaders in the work of ministry, building up the body. Making disciples of all nations extends beyond the space where the group meets, and involves friends and new people.

Group members serving in the ministry of the body of Christ will increase when group leaders and members encourage them to do so. We encourage the members of the group I attend (Circle of Friends) to serve in the church. Some are deacons. Some serve on committees or teams. And many have gone out of the group to serve as group leaders and workers in ministries for preschoolers, children, students, and adults.

When someone goes out of the Circle of Friends, we don't stop caring for them. We send them out with prayer. They continue to receive our prayer emails and invitations to our events (fellowships, projects, and meals). Because care and relationships with an adult group continue, I find that workers in younger ages don't seem to burn out as quickly. And when they do leave their posts, they tend to stay connected and often return to the Circle of Friends.

WHEN SOMEONE GOES OUT OF THE CIRCLE OF FRIENDS, WE DON'T STOP CARING FOR THEM.

As group members serve the body of Christ beyond the group, they gain relationships and opportunities to pray and care for others and to have others care for them. They gain additional avenues for sharing their giftedness and experiences with the larger body of Christ.

In addition, there are many events and ministries in our churches where members of an adult or student group can invest, whether on an ongoing or a one-time basis. There are more opportunities than I can list. Consider these as starter ideas:

- VACATION BIBLE SCHOOL. Decorate, lead an age group, provide recreation, lead the crafts, distribute flyers, fix the snacks, provide a teacher green room, follow up with unchurched families, and so much more.

- BLOCK PARTY OR HARVEST FEST. Help set up the event, set up a booth, provide food or water, register guests for a giveaway, provide music or entertainment, ask for prayer requests, pray with people, share the gospel, etc.

- CHURCH WORKDAY. Clean or paint the church, do landscaping, beautify the playground, clean windows, etc.

- SINGLE MOTHERS' OIL CHANGE. Do simple vehicle maintenance for single mothers, provide snacks, ask for prayer requests and pray, provide Bibles, share the gospel, etc.

- MAKING ENGLISH A SECOND LANGUAGE. Help those who have moved here to learn English, provide childcare and snacks, etc.

What would happen to the relationships in your group if you served together for church projects? As you plan and work together, you strengthen relationships. You laugh and work together and get to know one another in ways otherwise not possible. Raise the value of group members serving together in the church. Let me challenge you as a group leader to count and seek to increase annually the number of those involved in serving in the church.

SERVING IN THE COMMUNITY AND THE WORLD

Jesus commanded His disciples (us) to make disciples of all nations. The work of ministry for the body of Christ does not all take place in the church building during group time or worship. Adult and student group members help the church carry out the important work of relationships, care, witnessing, and disciple-making as they go into the community and the world. They do so in every phase of life: at work, school, home, and in the marketplace.

When the group's care team shares a friend's need from the community, state, nation, or world, you tap into the giftedness of those God has gathered as part of the group. You raise the value of serving. You give expression to group members' care. And along the way through discussion, planning, and serving together, you strengthen relationships with each other.

I mentioned in chapter 11 that the point of projects is to strengthen relationships, reconnect absentees, and connect with new friends as you work or serve together or help a person or organization in need. My point here is to remind us that serving provides opportunities to involve absentees and new friends. Allow me to offer an illustration of how this might work and why it is important.

Your group decides to invest a Saturday in working on a Habitat for Humanity home. Habitat for Humanity is a non-profit organization that helps families build and improve places to call home. They build strength, stability, and self-reliance through shelter (habitat.org).

Your group communicates with the local Habitat contact, chooses a Saturday, announces the plans a month early, and reminds members weekly to invite absentees and friends. The care team provides invitation cards for group members to take to friends. Care team members also assign absentees to those attending to extend invitations for participation.

On the day of the serving project, eight regular attenders along with two absentees and two friends join the work. As you work, you talk, laugh, and get to know one another. At the end of the day, you are tired, but you each have a sense of satisfaction from having helped a family move closer to being in their home. And your caring invitations to serve result in Bible study group attendance increasing by one absentee and one friend. Imagine the conversation on the day following the Habitat project!

ACTS 1:8 IDEA

What might happen if you invited group members to join you in something called the Acts 1:8 Challenge? Think about ways relationships can grow with members, absentees, and friends as you serve together in your Jerusalem (your community), Judea (your city or county), Samaria (your state or nation), and the uttermost parts of the world (another country).

Have you been on a mission trip? It is life-changing. Serving projects can be life-changing as well. Guide your group to establish ongoing relationships rather than one-time projects.

What if you challenged your group to plan and serve annually in ongoing ways in (choose one of each pair): (1) your Jerusalem or Judea, and (2) your Samaria or the uttermost. I have heard of groups that strive to serve at all four levels.

WITH THE LORD'S HELP, LIVES WILL CHANGE.

Can you imagine the relationship-building and life-changing impact on your group as you involve absentees and friends? Can you imagine the impact of your care on those you serve? With the Lord's help, lives will change. May our service tell Him and them, "We care!"

SECTION SIX: SERVING SOLO AND AS A GROUP

REFLECTION QUESTIONS

1. CHAPTER 14: What can you do to increase the involvement of members in serving in the group?

2. CHAPTER 14: Calculate your group's span of care (number of group members including absentees divided by the number of care team members). If the number is five or greater, what can you do to increase serving on the care team to improve your span of care?

3. CHAPTER 15: How many group members serve in some capacity in the church (beyond the group)? How could you lead more of them to serve in the church in the year ahead?

4. CHAPTER 15: How could your group increase awareness of needs and opportunities for service in your community and the world?

5. CHAPTER 15: How could implementing the Acts 1:8 Challenge help you to involve more members, absentees, and friends in serving in the months and years ahead?

SECTION SEVEN: USING CARE LISTS

After the Bible study group leaders meeting, Mike stopped Buster and said, "Buster, because the church has grown, I see the need for moving to the new membership software. But getting everyone in my group to update their contact information is going to be a lot of work and will take a lot of time."

Buster replied, "Mike, I think you will be surprised at how much attender information you will get quickly and easily when your group gathers. This week, the church office will provide contact information printed for every member with needed information highlighted. Then if your care team asks group members to contact absentees, I believe you will have ninety-five percent of the information complete within a couple of weeks."

Mike asked, "Do you really believe so?"

Buster said, "Yes. Your group has great relationships with your absentees. I think it will be yet another reason to show your absentees that you care."

Buster added, "And during this month, ask your group members to contact your friends as well. We are not asking you to report friend contact information to the office, but your group needs updated information for friends as well."

Mike replied, "That makes sense. We will get it done. Thanks!"

CHAPTER 16

MEMBER CARE LIST

In chapter 6, I shared the importance of gathering and updating contact information. The information we gather from members (including absentees) forms our member care list. The contact information we gather from our friends forms our friends care list. Notice the key word, *care*. I will focus on the friend care list in chapter 17. In this chapter, I will address the member care list.

There are many ways to collect and store member contact information. In this age of phones and computers, digital lists help us access and update information anytime, anywhere. There are many apps available to help, of varying cost and function. These options don't require print copies of the list. But it may, however, be convenient to collect registration information from guests and new members on a printed form.

Simple digital alternatives include using Excel (numbers) or tables in Word (pages). And it is always possible to collect and file paper copies of contact information. With these options, sharing print copies of the member care list may be necessary.

CONTACT INFORMATION TO REQUEST

I recommend collecting only information that you will use. For instance, if you never intend to celebrate wedding anniversaries, don't request that information. Here is a common list of types of contact information that may be useful in providing care for members and absentees:

- First and last name
- Preferred name
- Address (street, city, state, zip code)
- Phone number (work, home, cell, text, including area code)
- Email address
- Preferred contact method (phone, text, email)
- Social media accounts
- Employer
- Birth date
- Anniversary date
- Christian (yes or no)
- Church member (where)
- Parents (if information is about a minor)
- School grade (if information is about a minor)

COLLECTING THE CONTACT INFORMATION

When you collect contact information from every new group member, the task shifts to keeping that list updated. I have, however, observed many groups that have no formal member care list. And many others have a list with much missing information. That means that communication and care in time of need may not be possible.

If the missing information is from a small number of individuals, request the same information you would request from new members (use the same form or app). Since many people tune out mass appeals, request this information privately to garner better results. Follow up until you have received the information.

If the missing information is from most of the group, print the information you have and highlight the information you are seeking (verbally or with a highlighter on the form). Ask everyone to review the information, providing the missing information. Do this during a group session when you expect to have the greatest participation. Then follow up with those who are absent as soon as possible. Again, be persistent. Care depends on this information.

FOLLOW UP UNTIL YOU HAVE RECEIVED THE INFORMATION.

USING THE MEMBER CARE LIST

The value of the member care list is using it to mobilize care by members of the group. So whatever method you choose, your goal is to make it as user-friendly and accessible as possible. Teach the group how to access it and use it. Where possible, teach them how to update their own contact information when it changes. Ask them to inform you when they discover incorrect information for others.

Remember that multiple practice sessions using the member care list may help increase confidence and competence. Why is that important? We want members to be able to contact group members and absentees when assigned, and spontaneously. We can make a contact assignment by passing out a slip of paper with a name and contact information on it. But it is so much simpler to assign a name, knowing group members have access to updated contact information.

When the group has access to correct information, we can ask individuals, members of the care team, or the entire group to contact and care for a member or absentee in need or to celebrate a special day. We can do so by visit, phone, digital, or mail. If the group is in a closed group on social media or a dedicated app for the group, mobilizing care may be even simpler. But there are limits to every communication method. For instance, planning a surprise party for the group's leader when using a closed group or app may prove to be challenging.

SUBGROUP LISTS

When the number of group members increases to more than five, forming contact subgroups may facilitate communication, planning, and care. Creating a list of the group's care team is also beneficial. Doing so can streamline communication for planning and care. Other subgroups may also be desirable: serving or mission projects, event-planning teams, etc. Review all subgroups often to ensure they include the correct members.

ORGANIZING CARE GROUPS (IN LARGER GROUPS)

There are many wrong ways to organize care groups. We could organize by weight, height, IQ, or age. Or we could organize by frequency of attendance: dropouts, those who attend one week per month, two to three weeks per month, or four to five weeks per month. Finally, we could organize by length of time as a Christian: unsaved, less than a year, two to ten years, eleven to thirty years, or thirty-one-plus years. There are so many obvious problems with those choices.

In a group with fifteen people or more, Care Group Leaders (Appendix 3A) may be helpful to ensure that the span of care remains small enough for effective care. For care groups to work well, each group needs a balance of members. I like the categories used by Allan Taylor in *The Six Core Values of Sunday School,* pages 125-128. He uses these terms:

- TOUCH GROUP: those who attend up to six times a year.
- MINISTRY GROUP: those who attend seven to twenty-three times a year.
- CORE GROUP: those who attend twenty-four-plus times per year.

Allan suggests dividing members (including absentees) into these three categories. Then add one person from each category to each care group. Then add the second person from each category to the list. Repeat until you run out of names. I would add a fourth category to Allan's three: Care Group Leaders. Adding the leaders as a fourth category will make the Core Group list smaller. Put the leaders' names at the top of the list, and then follow Allan's directions.

Allan states, "This system evenly distributes all those in the Touch Group, Ministry Group, and Core Group into . . . Care Groups" (p. 127). This gives each care group a similar number of Core people to assist in providing care for the Ministry and Touch members. This is essential for care group effectiveness.

Since care groups pray together, care for one another, and challenge one another as disciples, I believe the ideal number in a care group is five or six, including the leader. My thinking revolves around the fact that everyone in a group of six participates. Keep in mind that a care group may also be an ideal unit to start a new Bible study group as the original group grows.

At the end of chapter 5, I mentioned the benefits of single-gender care groups in coed groups. If you keep couples together, it may be necessary for care groups to be larger. To form single-gender care groups in a coed group, you start with separate lists of males and females and follow the directions above.

As you can see, assignment in groups can be fluid. That will make your communication and care lists more challenging to keep up-to-date. But the benefits of the lists will be worth the effort.

AVOID DROPPING MEMBERS

Care should not stop when a member drops out. In fact, *every* absence should result in contact and care. Absentees will always appreciate care. For instance, if Betty is on vacation at the beach, she will know you care if you reach out by text to let her know you missed her and hope she is having a fun, relaxing time.

Help your group understand that it is their job to care for each other. If you don't know why members are out, expressing that you missed them and asking how you can pray for them will be appreciated. Ask group members to text, email, or call them. One idea is to take a picture of

CARE SHOULD NOT STOP WHEN A MEMBER DROPS OUT.

the group. Have everyone sign the lower half of an 8.5 x 11 sheet of paper. Then print the picture on the sheet, and mail it to the absentee with the message: "We missed you." Or ask everyone to send a postcard with a brief message.

If we contact absentees every week, we will never allow our contact information with them to get outdated. And our absentees will always know we care. Over time, relationships will deepen as we continue to express care.

Despite regular expressions of care, some absentees will become dropouts. They may experience illness, job-schedule change, care requirements for a loved one, conflict, or other situations. It is possible that the initial need for absence was only a few weeks, but now the habit to remain home is stronger than the habit to come. Even when the weeks of absence become months and the months become years, care should continue. We should never allow "out of sight, out of mind" to rule the day.

A member of a senior ladies group dropped out. Gay had been gone for months when her dad died. Because members had never stopped caring and Gay's name was still on the member care list, group members reached out in care and attended the funeral. It was during that time of need that Gay realized how much she missed the group, and she returned.

There are three main reasons to drop someone from our member care list. Review the following list:

1. The member *died*.

2. The member *moved* out of the ministry reach of the group and church. Do so only if it is too far for the member to return and too far for the group to provide care.

3. The member *joined* another group in your church or in another church. Notice that I did not say the member joined another *church*. Since we want them to experience the care of a group, we refuse to remove them from our member care list until they find another group.

Another reason to remove someone from your member care list is if the member asks you to remove them. To me, this request is a cry for help and prayer. It is difficult for me to remove them because I fear we will stop praying for the person.

One way to honor the request and to continue to pray is to remove all contact information for the person from our records (address, phone, email, and social media information). Ask members to do the same from personal lists or subgroups, unless there is a personal relationship with the individual separate from the group. Then each time you see the name (without contact information), stop and pray for the individual because you care.

CHAPTER 17

FRIEND CARE LIST

For several years, I have struggled with the term *prospect.* Disciples of Jesus need to care for and develop relationships with people in the world whether they join our groups or not. We do so because we have fallen in love with Jesus and want everyone to know Him and what He has done for them.

I fear that the term *prospect* may lead to a mindset that we only need to care for people who may be potential members for our group. Don't get me wrong. I believe in what God can do through a group that weekly gathers to meet Him in Bible study, that cares for one another, and that lives obediently as disciplemakers in the world.

But God loved the *world* so much (John 3:16) that He sent Jesus. We plant and water, but He sends the increase (1 Corinthians 3:7). We pray to the Lord of the harvest for workers (Matthew 9:38). We love our neighbors (Matthew 22:39). And we do our part along life's path to make disciples (Matthew 28:19-20). Our job is not to choose or select. Our job is to care and pursue, for Him.

Because I have struggled with the term *prospect,* I have renamed the classic term *prospect list* to *friend care list.* Do you notice the subtle difference? The friend care list focuses on our friends. And the focus of the list is to help our group to provide care for our friends.

CREATING A FRIEND CARE LIST

There are many advantages for gathering a contact list of our friends, including giving group members opportunities for prayer, care, and relational connection with our friends. In this book when I use the term *friend*, I include FRANs. *FRANs* is a term used by Elmer Towns in *FRANtastic Days: Reaching Your Friends, Relatives, Associates & Neighbors for Christ*. As the title suggests, *FRANs* is an acronym for friends, relatives, associates, and neighbors; the "s" makes the term plural. Associates include everyone else who is not a friend, relative, or neighbor.

The group's Friend Leader/Shepherd leads the group to develop a friend care list. There are many ways to accomplish this task. While you know your group better than I do, I want to emphasize the importance of the effort and recommend that you avoid rushing or shortcuts. Here are three methods, with the third method being my recommendation.

One method is to dedicate ten to fifteen minutes of a group session or event. Pass out index cards of four distinct colors (let's say yellow, pink, blue, and green). Explain that you need their help developing a friend care list. Hold up the yellow card and ask them to write down the name and contact information of a *friend* that the group can pray for, care for, and invite to your group events. Then hold up the pink card, and do the same, asking for the name and contact information of a *relative*. Then hold up a blue card for *associates* and then a green card for *neighbors* and do the same. Ask them to sign their cards. Collect the cards. Consolidate them into a list to make available to the group for review.

A second option is to pass out sheets of paper. Ask members to write *Friends* at the top and *Relatives* in the middle of the sheet's first side. Turn it over and have them write *Associates* at the top and *Neighbors* in the middle of the second side. Then give them the same explanation and walk them through each FRANs category. Have them sign their cards. Allow me to provide a warning. If you don't coach them toward giving you a name in each of the four categories, members will share only one name in one category.

The third option is the one I believe may provide the best results. Dedicate five minutes of four consecutive group sessions to do the following: Each week pray together before you begin. Then explain that you are developing a friend care list and need their help. You will use this list to pray for, care for, and invite friends to your events (socials, projects, and meals).

- **WEEK 1:** Pass out index cards; ask members to write the names and contact information (address, phone, email) of *friends* needing prayer, care, and connection; ask members to add their names and phone numbers on the index cards.

- **WEEK 2:** Pass out index cards; ask members to write the names and contact information (address, phone, email) of *relatives* needing prayer, care, and connection; ask members to add their names and phone numbers on the index cards.

- **WEEK 3:** Pass out index cards; ask members to write the names and contact information (address, phone, email) of *associates* needing prayer, care, and connection; ask members to add their names and phone numbers on the index cards.

- **WEEK 4:** Pass out index cards; ask members to write the names and contact information (address, phone, email) of *neighbors* needing prayer, care, and connection; ask members to add their names and phone numbers on the index cards.

Each week, request the same FRANs help from those who were absent. Also, look through the index cards (and emails from absent members) to determine if you have sufficient contact information. If you need more, contact the member who submitted the name to request the missing information.

When you have collected the FRANs information from members and absentees from the four weeks, consolidate and make the list available to group members in a similar mode (digital, app, or print) as your member care list. Have the group review the accuracy of the information.

WHAT DO WE DO WITH OUR FRIEND CARE LIST?

With the list, make plans for leading the group to care for and develop relationships with the friends on the list. How can you lead them in that direction? Start on the shallow end of the pool and lead them into the deeper water one step at a time. Here is an illustration:

- **WEEKS 1-4:** Start with praying for the friends, relatives, associates, and neighbors on the list.

- **WEEKS 3-6:** Ask group members to contact their FRANs to ask how they can pray for them. Then pray with them. If you discover a nonconfidential need with which the group may help, share it with the group and mobilize care.

- **WEEKS 5-8:** Follow up on prayer requests (this shows you care). Then ask again how you can pray. Then pray together.

- **WEEKS 7-10:** Invite the friend to a group event (social, project, or meal).

- **WEEKS 9-12:** Follow up on participation in the group

event. Ask how you can pray. Then pray together. If friends are unable to attend the group event, invite them to join you for a meal or a life event.

- **THEREAFTER:** Continue prayer, care, invitations, and ministry. Be consistent. Seek opportunities to care for them by sharing your testimony and the plan of salvation.

Do you see the intentional plan for developing relationships and expressing care to friends? This was an illustration, but I encourage you to make it your own. There are two reasons, however, to avoid lengthening the time between prayer, care, and invitations:

1. GROUP MEMBERS ARE DEVELOPING NEW HABITS OF CARE. Habits tend to require at least three continuous weeks to develop. Since these care habits are not daily, they will require a longer period of reinforcement as the group practices care expression.

2. NEW RELATIONSHIPS NEED GREATER ATTENTION. In my experience, the longer the time between caring contact, the less friends will feel that you care. We best express care weekly, or at most biweekly. In times of stress or need, care may need even more frequent expression.

See Appendices 3A and 3B for the job description of the Friend Care Leader and Friend Shepherd. This leader's job is not to care for everyone on the friend care list. The leader's job is to lead the *group* to care for those on the list. Working together with the group's care team, the Friend Leader/Shepherd will plan and promote group events (socials, projects, meals, and special studies) and support church events, encouraging members to care for and invite friends throughout the year.

CHAPTER 18

NEW MEMBERS: MOVING FROM FRIEND TO MEMBER

When we add new members, we add them to the member care list. It may involve moving them from the friend care list. What is the value of adding people to the list? Is it only to determine who is present and who is absent? No, it is so much more.

BENEFITS

Think about your group. What are the benefits that members gain by being part of your group? What do you do for those who are members of your group? Here are a few of my favorite things:

- We listen to and care for one another.

- We learn how to study God's Word together.

- We discover affinities (things in common) as we laugh, cry, and pray together.

- We realize we are not the only ones who are less than perfect.

- We connect with each other as we become friends and cheerleaders for one another.

- We develop caring, trusting relationships.

- We support and help one another in good times and in times of need.

- We serve each other and others together.

- We do life together and enjoy spending time together at Bible study, parties, projects, and meals.

- God allows us the privilege to walk with lost people who join us in meeting Him in Bible study, watching many of them accept a saving relationship with Christ.

- We watch the saved become disciples, and disciples become disciplemakers and leaders.

Why do we want to add people to our list? We want them to experience the same care and benefits we have experienced.

Do you want lost and unconnected friends to accept Jesus? I have asked more than 100 pastors over the last ten years how many lost people are saved within twelve months of attending a group. They have all replied with one of two answers: 50 percent or 100 percent accept Jesus within a year.

David Francis in *Connect*[3]*: The Power of One Sunday School Class* says, "The evidence is overwhelming: a person enrolled in Sunday School is about one hundred times more likely to receive Christ than a person who is not enrolled in a class or small group" (p. 11). Wow!

My experience is that this is true for small groups as well, when we invite lost friends to study the Bible with us. Do you want your friends to accept Jesus? Ask them if you can add them to your member care list. Because you care for them, you want them to know Jesus. Share Jesus with them and invite them to join your group for Bible study.

Do you want a friend to experience the care of your group? Ask if you can add them to your list. Then care for them. Pray for them. Invite them to your events and group sessions.

Do your friends want to know more about the Bible and Jesus? Ask if you can add them. Help them to know how fun (and safe) your group sessions are. Help them to know how many of *your* questions have been answered there.

If your friends allow you to add them to your list, your job is to care for them like you care for members (or even better). If your friends were on your friend care list, move them from that list to your member care list. Then pray for them. Spend time with them in life and at Bible study and group events. Help in time of need.

ASKING FRIENDS ABOUT ADDING THEM TO THE MEMBER CARE LIST

There is nothing wrong with a member of the care team asking to add my friends. But in my experience, the best person to extend the invitation to my friends is me. My friends know and trust me. I know when my friends are ready. We have had interactions beyond group sessions and events. Ask your friends if you can add them to your list.

MY FRIENDS KNOW AND TRUST ME.

WHEN SHOULD I ASK IF I MAY ADD THEM?

When my friends are ready, I extend an invitation without any pressure. It is important, however, for me to resist a natural temptation to wait too long. I must avoid saying no for my friends. My job is just to ask.

Should I wait until my friends have attended the group three times to be sure they are serious? No, no, a thousand times no. Attending your Bible study group sessions is only one of the reasons for inviting your friends to enroll.

INVITE YOUR FRIENDS BECAUSE YOU CARE. There are even more reasons than the bulleted list shared earlier in this chapter. Invite your friends because you care and because you want them to experience the benefits you receive from being part of the group.

HOW DO I ASK THEM IF I MAY ADD THEM?

Terms matter. And some terms are confusing. I want to suggest that you avoid the term *join.* Friends may not understand the difference between *joining* your group and *joining* your church. Even the terms *enroll, enrollment,* and *enrolling* can be confusing. They may wonder why they are registering.

Instead, I want to offer a simple alternative. Ask friends if you can add them to your party, prayer, and care list. When they ask what is a "party, prayer, and care list," tell them it is a list of those your group invites to your parties and prays and cares for in time of need. Who would not want to be part of that list? (And isn't that what you do for your members?) Make sure to share details about your group's next event. And when the time is right, invite your friends to join the group for Bible study and be sure to share Jesus.

When your friends agree to be part of the list, share names and contact information with your care team. They will move your friends from the friend care list to the member care list. Share the good news with your group. Encourage group members to extend a welcome to your friends. Continue to contact, pray for and with, and care for your friends.

Consider the impact of asking your friends if you can add them to your care list. Hear what Thom and Sam Rainer had to say in *Essential Church? Reclaiming a Generation of Dropouts:* "So what have we discovered about Christians who hear good sermons each week, who are involved in a small-group Bible study, and who study the Bible on their own? We have found that such Christians rarely drop out. . . . And if they do, they are the most likely to return" (p. 199).

SECTION SEVEN: USING CARE LISTS

REFLECTION QUESTIONS

1. CHAPTER 16: Of the list of types of contact information we may request, which ones have you not collected? Would it be helpful to do so?

2. CHAPTER 16: What did you learn about using the member care list and about dropping members?

3. CHAPTER 17: Does your group have a friend care list? If you do, how do you use it? If not, what is the first step for your group to develop and use one?

4. CHAPTER 17: How could you lead group members to make contacts with friends each week? Would you increase member involvement in contacting friends if you asked them to text, email, or call friends when gathered?

5. CHAPTER 18: What would you add to the list of benefits members gain from being part of your group? Which benefits do your friends need?

6. CHAPTER 18: How does what you learned in this chapter differ from how your group adds new people to your member care list?

SECTION EIGHT: CARING IN TIME OF NEED

Mike ran into Buster on his way to worship. Mike said, "It happened again!"

Surprised, Buster asked, "What happened?"

Mike said, "We have another disgruntled member because no one visited while she was in the hospital – even though she told the group."

Buster replied, "You have a caring group. I'm sure it was not intentional. Work with your care team to apologize and resolve the situation. Mike, if you think it will help, I have an exercise designed for an entire group to train them to listen with care."

Mike said, "Yes, please share it. I think this is a teachable moment for us."

Buster said, "I will send it this afternoon. And I will also send information about organizing to meet needs. Timeliness of care is always essential."

Mike replied, "You got that right. I'll check my email later."

Buster said, "After you have read the information, share it with your care team. Let me know if you or they have any questions."

Mike said, "Will do. Thanks again, Buster!"

CHAPTER 19

DISCOVERING AND RESPONDING TO NEEDS OR CRISES

Even if your group has a full care team (see Appendices 3A and 3B), care requires the involvement of every group member. Members are the eyes, ears, and hands of care for the group. Each of them will have relationships and interactions with a unique set of people. This network of relationships in and out of the church will enable greater needs' discovery and response.

> **TESTIMONY:** WE HAD SOMEONE IN OUR GROUP FALL OFF A LADDER AND BREAK HIS FOOT. FOLLOWING HIS SURGERY, OUR GROUP FIXED MEALS FOR HIS FAMILY FOR ABOUT A WEEK. ANOTHER MAN IN OUR GROUP GAVE THE MAN WITH A BROKEN FOOT A RIDE TO WORK TO GIVE THE WIFE A BREAK. IT'S BEEN AWESOME TO SEE THE LORD BRING OUR GROUP CLOSER TOGETHER DURING THIS DIFFICULT TIME FOR THIS FAMILY.

Most of us have many conversations every day. We hear things in work and casual conversations that deserve our attention, care, and concern. The boss will be out for a week from outpatient surgery. Your best friend just heard that she will lose her job next week. Your neighbor's wheelchair-bound mother is coming to live with them, and your neighbor has no idea how to navigate the wheelchair up the seven steps into the house.

In each case, what was said was both a cry for help and a request for prayer. Were you listening? We should pay attention to this warning: *Hope delayed makes the heart sick* (Proverbs 13:12). Timeliness for our care matters. I recommend that you set aside time with group members for a special event to train them to practice intentional listening with care. If possible, record the training to share with those who cannot attend and those added to the group later.

ROLE PLAY: TRAIN THEM TO LISTEN WITH CARE

Ask the group's care team to plan a meal plus ninety minutes for the training. The meal will attract some to attend who might otherwise skip the training. Enlist people to help in as many ways as possible with the event. This is a proven way to increase participation in meetings and events.

Turn to Appendix 1 for Scenarios A, B, and C. The following is for your information only. *Do not announce the following:*

- Scenario A is designed so the listener can meet the need.

- Scenario B is designed so the group can meet the need.

- Scenario C is too large for the group alone and will require the help of the church and/or community to assist with the need.

Enlist three pairs of volunteers to read the assigned scenario with the group. Briefly review for the group the 3 levels of communication shared in chapter 7. Then, after each set of volunteers reads aloud the scenario, give a printed copy of the scenario to groups of four to six people with these five questions for discussion (fifteen to twenty minutes per scenario):

1. What need was presented in the scenario?

2. In what ways could the group member have improved listening, understanding the need, and expressing care?

3. What benefits might have resulted from the member writing down the need and asking to pray with the friend?

4. In what ways could it have helped to ask permission to share the need with the group?

5. What caring next steps can the member or group or church take?

After presenting and discussing the three role-plays, gather the larger group to debrief.

- Ask what they learned about: (1) listening, (2) expressing care, and (3) next steps.

- Ask how writing down the need or request shows you listened and care.

- Ask how praying together shows you care and God cares.

- Ask how their next conversations with friends will be different.

Listening and appropriate expressions of care, prayer, and follow-up are skills that grow with practice and intentionality. When we do so with members, absentees, and friends, everyone will know we are Jesus' disciples. Stop often to ask for testimonies of care. Consistently remind everyone, "We care."

SHARE NEEDS WITH THE CARE TEAM

When an individual alone can help with a discovered crisis or need, it is unnecessary to inform the care team. However, if the person receiving care is on the member care list or friend care list, sharing information with the care team can create awareness and prevent duplication of assistance.

We should connect information about meeting needs to the member's or friend's care list contact information (see chapters 6, 16, and 17). Record the date(s) for care, the person or group providing care, and a simple description of the care. The information should be readily available to the group's care team. Avoid reporting confidential information. In addition to preventing duplication of assistance, recording this information allows the care team to know the skills and relationships in the group. This knowledge may help with responding to future needs.

Reporting care efforts can enable the group to build on previous care. Ask members to complete and share a written report with the care team. Using a simple printed report form (see Appendix 2 for a sample) will facilitate collecting that information.

If you cannot add this information to a digital app of the member's or friend's contact information, collect written forms in a binder or type the information into a sharable document (Excel, Word, etc.). And always create a backup!

CHAPTER 20

ORGANIZING TO HELP IN TIME OF NEED OR CRISIS

A group with a care team increases the likelihood of discovering and responding to the crises and needs of members and friends. Training group members to listen, express care, and report needs prepares everyone to assist. The last step is organizing to respond when crises or needs occur.

Timeliness of care matters. If we don't hear about a need, we cannot pray or help. Because we care, we ask members, absentees, and friends for the privilege to pray with them and walk with them through challenging times. That means we ask members, absentees, and friends to think about us like family, and contact us early when dealing with crises and needs.

Because we care, we contact absentees and friends weekly. Contact enables us to express care by following up on previous needs, asking for prayer requests, and praying together. As a result, we discover any new needs and crises in a timely manner. Discovery allows the group to pray and provide care. The member in need stays connected because the group walked with him or her during the moment of need. The friend in need may decide to connect with events, Bible study, or Jesus because of the care. And as mentioned in chapter 6, regular communication helps us maintain updated contact information.

ORGANIZING THE GROUP FOR COMMUNICATION

When your group is not together for Bible study, how do you communicate with your group? Do you send out mass emails? Do you text or call everyone? Do you use an app like Line or Discord or a closed group on Facebook?

Who initiates the communication? If there is confusion here, the opportunity for delivering timely care may pass. Does the person discovering the need or crisis know to contact the person who initiates the communication? This requires training your care team along with every member of the group. Here are a couple of methods:

- CALL TREE. You can use a call tree: where one person calls two, those two call two others, etc. This method reduces calls by each person, but this method can become a communication bottleneck if the people we call don't respond. (To avoid any bottleneck, call the people on the list of the person who did not respond.) Two-way communication is best to confirm that the individual received the sent message and that the caller will make the next contact quickly.

- CARE TEAM. In a group with a fully functioning care team, the teacher or leader contacts care team members. Then care team members divide and contact other group members. Care Group Leaders (in larger groups) may also initiate contact with members of their groups. Care Group Leaders may even ask someone in their groups to contact half of the care group. This communication pattern strengthens the work of the team, their relationships with each other, and group members.

ORGANIZING FOR RESPONSE TO NEEDS OR CRISES

It is best to be prepared to respond. That means some decisions should be made before discovering needs or crises. To do so, I recommend gathering a needs or crises communication-and-response planning team.

If your group has a complete care team, the members of that team may be the most natural ones to form the planning team. If your group has no care team or only a partial one, gather two to four people to help you create a plan. If your group has five members or fewer, gather the entire group. If the group includes both genders, ensure there is a mix of males and females on the planning team.

Here are a few key questions to discuss as your team develops a communication-and-response plan:

COMMUNICATION

- When there is a need or crisis, to whom should the person discovering the need or crisis communicate first?

- Who determines whether to communicate the need or crisis to the care team, the entire group, or the church?

- What are some of the needs or crises about which group members should be informed and/or mobilized to care?

CARING RESPONSE

- Are there some needs or crises that can be handled by care team members on behalf of the group?

- What standard caring actions will the group take in the event of common needs or crises? (Setting standard actions ensures fairer and faster responses.)

- Is there a need to gather the group for a time of prayer related to the need or crisis?

- When a need or crisis occurs that is not on the common list, how will you quickly determine a response?

- What is the best way to collect money to prepare for responses to needs or crises requiring money (for cards, flowers, meals, utilities, etc.)?

POTENTIAL NEEDS OR CRISES

How will you respond in the following scenarios? Will your response be different for members and friends? Keep in mind that caring for our friends like they are family may result in greater connection, group attendance, and salvation.

Consider your opportunities to respond with care to the following needs or crises of members and friends:

- DEATH of a member or friend; a close family member (spouse, child, parent, etc.); or an extended family member (aunt, uncle, grandparent, etc.).

- SICKNESS OR OUTPATIENT SURGERY of a member or friend or a close family member.

- INPATIENT SURGERY WITH HOSPITALIZATION of a member or friend or a close family member.

- RETURN HOME FROM THE HOSPITAL by a member or friend.
- CHILDCARE NEED during a doctor's appointment by a member or friend.
- TRANSPORTATION NEED to church or a doctor's appointment by a member or friend.
- LACK OF INCOME because off work for a few weeks by a member or friend.
- LOST JOB by a member or friend.
- INABILITY TO PAY UTILITY BILLS by a member or friend.

> **TESTIMONY:** A GROUP MEMBER HAD A BABY, AND WE ORGANIZED MEALS FOR THEIR FAMILY USING MEAL TRAIN. (CHECK OUT HTTPS://WWW.MEALTRAIN.COM.) WE ALSO HAD CHURCH MEMBERS HELP THEM MOVE THE SAME WEEK AS THE BIRTH OF THE BABY.

Do you see the opportunity for expression of care in these situations? Do you see how friends can fall in love with a group that cares for them in these times of need or crisis? If you are prepared for these scenarios, care can be quicker. Group members may even arrive at the hospital before the pastor. And making these decisions now will help in times when an unexpected need or crisis occurs – and it will!

> **TESTIMONY:** ONE OF OUR LADIES HAD NO FAMILY AND BECAME QUITE ILL FOR MONTHS. OUR GROUP CLEANED HER APARTMENT, PROVIDED MEALS AND TRANSPORTATION TO APPOINTMENTS, AND CARED FOR HER CAT WHEN SHE WAS IN THE HOSPITAL AND REHAB FOR FOUR MONTHS.

After your planning team has developed a plan, share it with the group. Ask them to review it, ask questions, and make suggestions. The idea is to improve the plan and for the group to own the plan. This effort is yet another way to say, "We care."

After responding to the group's first need or crisis, debrief the group's response. Tweak the plan as needed. Again, inform the group and seek their feedback. Strive for continual improvement of your plan and your care, because your care will show you are Jesus' disciples.

COLLECTING MONEY FOR CARE

When a need or crisis occurs, will you need to gather as a group to collect money to help? The group I attend, the Circle of Friends, passes a box around once a month. We contribute because we know the many good things for which our money has provided care: grief cards, flowers, Gideon Bibles, meals, rent, utilities, wheelchair repair, and more.

THE POINT IS TO BE PREPARED TO RESPOND WITH CARE IN A TIMELY WAY TO THE NEEDS AND CRISES OF MEMBERS AND FRIENDS.

Because we know the good, everyone is eager to add what cash (or check) they can. When the money is low, we pass around the box more frequently. When there is plenty of money, the box may not be passed around for a couple of months.

Some groups have checking accounts. Today, there are plenty of methods for groups to fund help. Set up an app. There is often a cost for this convenience, but it is worth it for many groups. The method does not matter. The point is to be prepared to respond with care in a timely way to the needs and crises of members and friends.

SECTION EIGHT: CARING IN TIME OF NEED

REFLECTION QUESTIONS

1. CHAPTER 19: How could you lead even more members to communicate needs discovered among members and friends? When needs or crises occur, how could you lead even more members to assist?

2. CHAPTER 19: How might the "Listen with Care" training event help your group with members, absentees, and friends?

3. CHAPTER 19: What are the benefits of recording ministry contact results with members and friends? How could you start or improve your group's process for recording contacts?

4. CHAPTER 20: When your group is not together, how do you communicate needs or crises of members and friends? Who initiates the communication?

5. CHAPTER 20. How would your group benefit from a needs or crisis communication and response planning session? Which of the list of questions would most benefit your group?

6. CHAPTER 20: Of the list of Potential Needs or Crises, which is your group least prepared to respond to in a timely manner? Why?

SECTION NINE:
BECOMING KNOWN FOR OUR CARE

After the meeting of Bible study group leaders and care team members, Mike stopped Buster and said, "Buster, I want to thank you for inviting me and my care team to share. I was a little intimidated when you enlisted me, but I have to say that I had a lot of fun tonight."

Buster replied, "Mike, your group's care made you the obvious choice for encouraging other groups to improve or start their care journey. I really liked how your care team jumped in."

Mike smiled and said, "Yeah, that was my favorite part. They were so excited when I asked them to help me. All I had to do was get out of the way."

Buster said, "Their passion for relationships and care is contagious. They shared perfect testimonies and stories. And I really like what your new member, Frank, had to say about why he joined your group and accepted Christ."

Mike replied, "Jesus was right when he said, *'By this everyone will know that you are my disciples, if you love one another.'* I memorized that verse during our journey."

Buster said, "Please thank your team for sharing tonight."

Mike replied, "Count on it. I bet they're already planning a celebration party. Thanks!"

CHAPTER 21

CREATING MOVEMENT: GETTING STARTED

By now, you understand our motivation for care. We care because Jesus cares. We care because He is the Shepherd-Owner of the sheep. We care because He commanded His disciples (us) to care like He cared. And when we care like He did, the world will know we are His disciples.

You now have a vision of what care looks like. Vision helps us stretch and move beyond current reality. As a result of the vision, you can see the goal. Without a finish line, it is difficult to run a race. In fact, it is difficult even to start the race.

God has chosen you to run the race. God has given you the gifts and abilities to run well. This race, however, will require encouragement because it is a marathon requiring endurance. To do so, God has surrounded you with cheerleaders who run the race with you. With clear motivation, vision, calling, ability, and encouragement, you must decide, you must make a commitment, to run the race. Will you? Will they?

Will you prepare well so you can run well? Will you help one another fight fatigue and discouragement to reach the finish line? Will you pray to the Lord of the harvest that He will surround you with God-called workers? Will you gather the workers He sends to pray, plan, care, and lead well, setting an example for others?

If you said yes, that is the first step toward starting. Without that start, there can be no movement or momentum. Congratulations on responding to the Lord's invitation to care for His sheep. Congratulations on making the decision, the commitment! May the Lord be honored. May He bless your efforts!

I'M COMMITTED; NOW WHAT?

Stop doing your work alone! This is God's work; you cannot do it without Him. Many have tried and failed. The work also requires the disbursed gifts of the body (Romans 12:3-5). You may be able to solo small portions of the work in the short run, but you will never complete the care marathon without help.

STOP DOING YOUR WORK ALONE!

Daniel Edmonds, my peer at the Alabama State Board of Missions, has a saying he uses in many contexts: "Start small. Do it right. Build it strong." Most of us believe we can skip the "start small" part. Laying the foundation is not glamorous, but it is essential to what we are building.

The same is true for relationships and care. Take the time to build them right. When we rush, we risk everything we do. Care is too important to do poorly. Remember what our Lord said: *"By this everyone will know that you are my disciples, if you love one another."*

STEPS TO START WELL

I want to offer several steps for launching the start of your care journey. Building on your commitment and recognition that you cannot do this work alone, begin the journey with these steps:

- PURSUE A FRESH RELATIONSHIP WITH THE LORD DAILY. How can you follow where He leads if you don't spend time with Him? How can you reflect His love if your love has grown cold? Set aside time daily in His Word and prayer. Don't skip this step!

- PRAY. Listen to Him in His Word and respond to what He says in prayer. Follow where He leads. Ask for wisdom and greater understanding of His love. Ask Him to send workers for the harvest. Seek His help in recognizing the workers He will send. When you add group members and care team members, lead them to join you in praying.

- BEGIN MODELING CARE. Don't wait for others to do the work of care. Begin now. Visit, call, and send texts. Pray with people. Listen well. Care. Be a friend. Your caring example matters!

- SHARE WHY CARE IS IMPORTANT. This book has shared many reasons why care is important. Foremost is Jesus' example. He dwelt among us, lived a sinless life, and took our place on the cross to restore our relationship with God. His teaching and example demonstrate His compassion and care. Add His example to His commands for us to love one another and make disciples of all nations. Second, remind them that our group, church, and world need care that looks like Jesus' care. Third, share your own journey of care. Why does it matter to you? Why do you care?

- ENLIST A CARE TEAM. Pray. Observe. When He lays someone on your heart, ask the person, "Will you help me?" Do life and ministry together. When the time is right, ask the person to serve, sharing about your prayer, observations, and belief in their competence. Don't rush enlistment of the care team. As you enlist each person, ask them to model care.

- GATHER FOR A CARE TEAM PLANNING RETREAT. You don't have to have a full care team enlisted to plan. The value of the retreat is ownership of the plan. Seek their involvement and input throughout the retreat. You will want to include some key planning steps to the retreat agenda: (1) evaluate the current reality of relationships and care; (2) identify needs; (3) determine priorities – what is most important or where do we start; (4) set goals – focus on the top three priorities; and (5) make plans to accomplish the goals – for the top one or two priorities. Before the retreat ends, schedule progress meetings to check on progress and evaluate or adjust plans as needed. Eat. Have fun. Practice care – even during the retreat! Repeat the retreat annually.

- DETERMINE THE PLACE TO START. If you followed the agenda steps I offered, step 3 helped you determine where to start. Those priorities with their goals and plans are where to start. I do offer two suggestions. First, work to ensure a small, early success. This will encourage the care team and group. Second, think in terms of moving your group from shallow water to deeper water in relationships and expressing care. If you jump too deep too early, the group may not be ready, resulting in discouragement from wasted time and effort. Continue to do it right and build it strong!

- EVALUATE REGULARLY. Never rest on your history. Relationships and care are in a constant state of ebb and flow. Conflict happens. New relationships begin. Gather your care team to evaluate everything you do.

ENCOURAGE THEM!

Never underestimate the power of an encouraging word. Listen and observe well. Catch members doing something good; affirm them. Model care in your Bible study lessons and group events. Ask people to share testimonies of giving and receiving care.

When you meet with your care team, ask them to share recent stories about relationships and care. Encouragement is one of the best ways we can ensure care momentum. Doing so says, "I care."

ENCOURAGEMENT IS ONE OF THE BEST WAYS WE CAN ENSURE CARE MOMENTUM.

I want to recommend a valuable resource. It could be helpful for your care team or entire group. The book is *The Five Love Languages* by Gary Chapman. Check out the web page focused on friendships: https://5lovelanguages.com/start/friendships/. The five love languages are words of affirmation, quality time, physical touch, acts of service, and receiving gifts. When we express these love languages in appropriate ways, encouragement can be even more meaningful.

CHAPTER 22

THE IMPACT OF CARE

HIS LOVE IMPACTS OUR CARE

Care is a choice to invest in others. Care requires a decision to sacrifice myself and my time, resources, and agenda for another person. That was what Jesus did for you and me. In Philippians 2:5-8, Paul writes, *Adopt the same attitude as that of Christ Jesus, who, existing in the form of God, did not consider equality with God as something to be exploited. Instead, he emptied himself by assuming the form of a servant, taking on the likeness of humanity. And when he had come as a man, he humbled himself by becoming obedient to the point of death— even to death on a cross.*

Like Christ, we must humble ourselves to express care. We do not wait for others to care for us; we must take the first step in doing so. In Matthew 7:12, Jesus said, *"Therefore, whatever you want others to do for you, do also the same for them, for this is the Law and the Prophets."*

To make the choice to serve and care for others before others care for us requires devotion to God. Responding to a question about the greatest commandment, in Mark 12:30-31 Jesus said, *"Love the Lord your God with all your heart, with all your soul, with all your mind, and with all your strength. The second is, Love your neighbor as yourself. There is no other command greater than these."*

Where in life and even in the church do we learn to love God like that? Where are we encouraged to love others like Jesus did? The best place I know to practice that kind of love is with a small group of caring believers who open God's Word together to hear and obey what He has to say.

When we love the Lord with all our heart, mind, soul, and strength, only then can we fully love our neighbor and even ourselves. As we learn to obey Him by loving one another, others come to see that we are His disciples. That happens because our care reflects His love.

OUR CARE CAN CHANGE THE WORLD

Follow this logic. God is love (1 John 4:8). And *the fruit of the Spirit is love, joy, peace, patience, kindness, goodness, faithfulness, gentleness, and self-control* (Galatians 5:22-23). Jesus commanded us to love one another, *"as I have loved you."*

Our care is revolutionary. His love calls us to live out the fruit of the Spirit. What does fruit-filled care look like? Consider this:

- It is agape, self-sacrificing love.

- It is joyful even in trials.

- It is peaceful even in turmoil.

- It is patient in a world that hates to wait.

- It is kind even when others are hateful.

- It is good in the face of evil.

- It is faithful to Him even when others ridicule.

- It is gentle and strong even when pushed around.

- It maintains self-control by choosing to let Him control.

That care is so different from the love of the world that it catches people's attention. It is so unique that they ask questions. It is so compelling that they ask questions about our care and about Jesus. They can tell we are His disciples.

When our Bible study group cares for Him and each other, His love spills beyond the walls where we gather. It touches family and friends. It spreads to school and work. Every act and conversation at play and in the marketplace puts His love on display.

WHEN OUR BIBLE STUDY GROUP CARES FOR HIM AND EACH OTHER, HIS LOVE SPILLS BEYOND THE WALLS WHERE WE GATHER.

Are we perfect in our expression of care? No, we are forgiven sinners, but His love calls us to try repeatedly. With His help, we seek to be clean mirrors (James 1:23-25) who obey and reflect as much of His light and love as possible.

What is the potential of our care? How far can it go? Consider this:

- Our care looks more like His as we practice that love with each other.

- Some step forward to provide care leadership and call others to care.

- Care spills beyond our meeting space into relationships on our journey in the community and the world.

- We share His love with friends and provide help in time of need.

- Jesus attracts our friends and people on our path; some accept Him as Savior and Lord and join us on the journey.

- Through caring events, lives encounter His love all over the community, county, state, nation, and world.

- Because of His love, the lost are saved. The saved become disciples. Disciples become disciplemakers. Love spreads.

WHAT'S NEXT?

How far could the care of one group go? Could one child accept Jesus? Could that child be the next Billy Graham? Could your care lead a family to become disciples of our Lord? Could that family become missionaries? What about a trailer park or subdivision? Could your care result in life change and crime reduction? What about a people group or nation? Could they stand before the Lord, giving Him thanks for sending you to care for them?

What will you do with what you have read? What is your next step? What steps will you lead your group to take? Pray. Make a commitment. Share your commitment with someone who will pray with you and help you take the next steps. The Lord will be pleased. You will be blessed and a blessing as you love Him and care for His sheep. Dare to express, "I care!"

As you undertake the journey of care, my prayer for you is the benediction from the book of Hebrews: *Now may the God of peace, who through the blood of the eternal covenant brought back from the dead our Lord Jesus, that great Shepherd of the sheep, equip you with everything good for doing his will, and may he work in us what is pleasing to him, through Jesus Christ, to whom be glory for ever and ever. Amen* (Hebrews 13:20-21, NIV).

SECTION NINE: BECOMING KNOWN FOR OUR CARE

REFLECTION QUESTIONS

1. CHAPTER 21: Are you committed to leading your group to care well for each other and for friends? With whom can you share this commitment to provide encouragement and support?

2. CHAPTER 21: Are you willing to stop working and caring alone as you build a great care team and caring group? How can you get more group members involved?

3. CHAPTER 21: Of the "Steps to Start Well," on which do you need help? Why?

4. CHAPTER 22: As we express care in life today, focusing on which three of the fruit of the Spirit will make our love more like Jesus?

5. CHAPTER 22: On your journey toward caring for each other and for friends, what is the next step for you and your group? Write out your plan.

APPENDIX I

SCENARIO A

After lunch on Friday, Jenny, the manager of a local pharmacy, calls Charice into her office. They are in the same Bible study group.

Jenny: Charice, I need you to cover things here for me next week. Can you do that?

Charice: Of course. What's up?

Jenny: I will have my gallbladder removed on Monday morning. I am a little anxious, but they say I should be able to return to work the week after.

Charice: Wow, Jenny, I didn't know. You know you can trust me. Is there anything out of the ordinary happening here next week?

Jenny: Normal routine here. You should have smooth sailing.

Charice: How did you know you had a problem with your gallbladder?

Jenny: The main symptom was abdominal pain, usually in the evening, after eating certain foods for many months. I finally said it was enough.

Charice: That explains why you never seem sick here. I hope things go great.

Jenny: If you have any questions, you have my cell number. Avoid calling Monday for obvious reasons. Thanks, Charice!

SCENARIO B

Bob and Frank work in different departments of the same plant. They are in the same Bible study group. Frank called Bob the next morning after hearing about his accident at work.

Frank: Bob, this is Frank. I heard about your fall. How are you doing?

Bob: Hey, Frank! Yesterday was rough, but I am feeling better today. They say it will be six to eight weeks before I can return to work.

Frank: I'm glad you feel better. I think I'd go stir-crazy if I had to stay home for that long. Is there anything you need me to bring you from the plant?

Bob: I don't think so, but I'll let you know. I need to sign some papers, but I think everything will be digital. I think Gabriela already talked to your wife about picking up my truck tomorrow.

Frank: In no time you will be back on your feet. But Gabriela has a big job ahead of her taking care of you and the twins. On the bright side, you get to watch Valentina and Rob grow.

Bob: Yeah, that is a silver lining. If you know any teens at church that could mow the grass, let me know. Hey, Frank, my pain med is making me groggy. I am going to lie down. Thanks for calling.

Frank: Good talking to you, Bob. Take it easy. We'll visit again soon.

SCENARIO C

Maria and Raven live on the same street and teach at the local elementary school. They both have daughters in fourth grade who ride bikes together. Maria's family has attended a cookout with Raven's Bible study group. Raven calls Maria on Saturday.

Raven: Maria, I heard about the fire. Are the three of you okay?

Maria: We're shaken up, but we made it out alive. I don't know what we are going to do. We lost everything.

Raven: I am so sorry. Where did you stay last night?

Maria: We stayed at the local motel. It's a little run-down. We were so exhausted, but none of us slept much.

Raven: I can imagine. Did you have insurance?

Maria: Yes, thankfully we're covered. We paid for it last year before Tony lost his job. It has been a rough six months, and this didn't help!

Raven: I'm glad you had insurance. I hope they move fast for you.

Maria: Jim, the agent, has already called. We are meeting him at the house and then going to his office in a few minutes.

Raven: Oh. Then I better let you go. Maria, let us know how we can help. Talk to you later.

Maria: Thanks for calling. Later.

APPENDIX 2

MEMBER AND FRIEND CARING CONTACT REPORTS

MEMBER - Name _____ Date _____

Person Contacted _____

Method of Contact: _____ Visit _____ Phone _____ Email _____ Text

Result of Contact (What need was discovered? How did you provide care? How can we provide care?)

FRIEND - Name _____ Date _____

Person Contacted _____

Method of Contact: _____ Visit _____ Phone _____ Email _____ Text

Result of Contact (What need was discovered? How did you provide care? How can we provide care?)

APPENDIX 3A

SUNDAY SCHOOL CLASS CARE TEAM
JOB DESCRIPTIONS

TEACHER AND APPRENTICE

Every teacher should pursue personal improvement as well as invest in training an apprentice. The apprentice needs to know not only how to teach but also how to care for and lead the group. When ready, the apprentice will either leave the group to start another group or will take over the current group when the teacher goes out to start another one.

After a season of prayer, the teacher and apprentice enlist the group's care team (see chapter 5 for enlistment help). In a student group, all care team members except the teacher and apprentice will be teens. When you enlist, train, and lead teens well, they are as effective as adults. It is important to be patient in discovering and mobilizing the right team members.

The teacher and apprentice gather the team to make plans. This often requires an annual retreat with the group's care team for prayer and planning. In addition, the team will plan regular progress-update meetings throughout the year.

The teacher and apprentice lead the care team to carry out those plans. The apprentice (once enlisted) may provide leadership and care for part of the care team while the teacher provides leadership and care for the rest of the care team. They trust and empower the team and group members to carry out plans. The teacher and apprentice support the work and the care team with their words, example, and involvement because modeling care is always the best way!

MEMBER CARE LEADER (MEMBER LEADER)

LEAD THE GROUP TO . . .

- **RECOGNIZE THE NEED FOR CARE.** Discuss member care, and *own* the responsibility. Enlarge the group's understanding about the need for care.

- **PRAY.** Pray together, in pairs and solo. Pray during group time and between sessions. Pray for physical, spiritual, and life needs and concerns. Share nonconfidential requests so others may pray.

- **MAKE WEEKLY CARE CONTACTS.** Assign members to contact members and absentees to express care. Share group plans and lessons. Ask for prayer requests. Pray together. Call for and record reports of caring contacts. Share discovered needs.

- **ORGANIZE TO MEET NEEDS.** Gather a team (Care Group Leaders in larger groups) to develop a strategy. This includes a plan for communication and response to discovered needs and crises.

- **PLAN OR CONDUCT SOCIALS, PROJECTS, AND MEALS.** Work with the Friend Leader to plan one of each event quarterly. Invite members, absentees, and friends. Plan conversation and care.

- **STRENGTHEN CONNECTIONS.** Notice when a group member has fewer than five friends in the group. Ask faithful attenders to invest additional time and attention with those individuals.

- **MAINTAIN GOOD RECORDS.** Develop and maintain the member care list. Record attendance and contact results weekly. Notice attendance change patterns. Ask members to verify address, phone, and email regularly. This may or may not be with the assistance of a secretary.

- **HESITATE TO DROP ANYONE.** Drop people from your member care list *only* if they die, move beyond ministry reach, or join another group (in your church or another).

FRIEND CARE LEADER (FRIEND LEADER)

LEAD THE GROUP TO...

- **PRAY.** Pray for the people-group assignment of your group; for lost and unenrolled people; and for group actions to identify, care for, and reach friends.

- **DEVELOP A FRIEND CARE LIST.** Ask for the names of FRANs (friends, relatives, associates, and neighbors) in your people-group assignment, people not enrolled in a group. Develop a plan to pray for and contact FRANs two to four times monthly. Update the list monthly.

- **PLAN AND INVITE FRIENDS TO FELLOWSHIPS, MEALS, AND PROJECTS.** Work with the Member Leader to plan one of each quarterly; make events fun and easy for people to get acquainted; before events end, invite everyone to the Bible study session.

- **ASSIGN CONSISTENT CARING CONTACTS WITH FRIENDS.** Follow up on previous prayer requests; share group plans for lessons and group events; ask how you can pray for the friend and his or her family; and pray together. Report nonconfidential requests.

- **SEND ELECTRONIC REMINDERS ABOUT GROUP PLANS.** To support caring contacts, communicate group plans by email, text, and social media.

- **WORK WITH GREETERS TO ENSURE POSITIVE FIRST IMPRESSIONS.** SEE THE JOB DESCRIPTION FOR GREETER.

- **INVITE FRIENDS AND GUESTS TO ENROLL.** Ask if you can add them to the care list for parties, prayer, and care. Pray for and set a God-sized new-member goal.

- **OFFER TESTIMONY PRACTICE.** Lead members to write out their salvation testimony. Ask them to share it in pairs, with family, with the entire group, and then with friends on life's path.

GREETERS

LEAD THE GROUP TO...

- **WELCOME.** Welcome members and guests. Get to know them. Listen well and pronounce names correctly. Ask guests if you may add them to the group care list.

- **REGISTER.** Seek guest contact information from the guest or the church welcome team. Ask members and guests to complete name tags to learn names.

- **ASSIST.** Introduce guests to the leader and group, calling guests by name. Sit with guests and share your Bible and curriculum.

- **GUIDE.** At session end, assist guests to find children, restrooms, and the sanctuary. Introduce guests to others in worship. After worship, thank the guest, ask if they have any questions, and introduce them to the pastor.

- **FOLLOW UP.** Use information from the registration card to make a brief call within three days to: (1) thank the guest for attending, (2) share upcoming group plans, (3) answer questions, (4) ask for prayer requests, and (5) pray together. If guests did not agree to be added to the group care list that day, add them to the friend care list.

SECRETARY

SUPPORT THE CARE TEAM WITH...

- **RECORDS.** Maintain group records and prepare reports including enrollment, contact information, attendance, and friend contact information and caring contact results.

- **GOALS.** Track progress and share reports of attendance, contact, and enrollment goals with the group and others as requested.

- **ORDERS.** Request and disburse curriculum, resources, and supplies.

- **CHANGES.** Track and report member attendance and changes. Gather a weekly list of members and absentees needing additional contact or ministry.

- **REPORTS.** Receive weekly written reports about caring contacts with members and friends.

- **LISTS.** Assign friends and new group members to care groups. Maintain updated care group assignment lists.

- **UPDATES.** Update member and friend contact information (phone, address, email) regularly.

CARE GROUP LEADERS (IN LARGER GROUPS)

Care Group Leaders may help the teacher and care team in many ways. Here we will focus on the care side of the responsibility.

LEAD THE CARE GROUP TO . . .

- **WELCOME.** Welcome, get to know, and introduce care group members and guests.

- **REGISTER.** Ask guests to complete a registration form so you can thank them and follow up.

- **ENCOURAGE NAME TAGS.** Ask care group members and guests to wear name tags.

- **REQUEST CONTACT REPORTS.** Ask for reports about contacts with absentees and friends. Seek updates for contact information.

- **ASSIGN CONTACTS.** Assign contacts for absentees and friends.

- **PRAY.** Ask for prayer requests and pray for care group members, absentees, friends, and guests.

- **FOLLOW UP.** Follow up with guests during the next three days.

APPENDIX 3B

SMALL GROUP CARE TEAM
JOB DESCRIPTIONS

GROUP LEADER AND APPRENTICE

Effective small group leaders will pursue personal improvement as well as invest in training an apprentice. The apprentice needs to learn to facilitate a Bible study session as well as how to care for and lead the group. When ready, the apprentice will leave the group to start another group *or* assume leadership of the current group when the group leader goes out to start another one.

After a season of prayer, the group leader and apprentice enlist the group's care team (see chapter 5 for enlistment suggestions). In a student group, all care team members except the group leader and apprentice will be teens. When you enlist, train, and lead teens well, they are as effective as adults. It is important to be patient in discovering and mobilizing the right team members.

To increase the impact of the group, the group leader and apprentice gather the care team to make plans. This often requires an annual retreat with the team for prayer and planning. In addition, the team will plan update meetings throughout the year.

The group leader and apprentice lead the care team and group to carry out those plans. The apprentice (once enlisted) may provide leadership and care for a portion of the care team or group while the group leader provides leadership and care for the rest. These two entrust and empower the team and group to carry out plans, and they support the work of the care team with their words, example, and involvement. Modeling care is always the best way!

HOST

Every small group needs a host whether meeting in a home, church, or other location.

- **WELCOME.** The host will provide a warm welcome at the door, helping to set a family-feeling for the group's time together.
- **ASSIST.** The host will provide assistance for the group leader, apprentice, and home or business owner with the meeting and space.

MEMBER SHEPHERD

LEAD THE GROUP TO . . .

- **RECOGNIZE THE NEED FOR CARE.** Discuss member care, and *own* the responsibility. Enlarge the group's understanding about the need for care.

- **PRAY.** Pray together, in pairs and solo. Pray during group time and between sessions. Pray for physical, spiritual, and life needs and concerns. Share nonconfidential requests so others may pray.

- **MAKE WEEKLY CARE CONTACTS.** Assign members to contact members and absentees to express care. Remind them about group events. Ask for prayer requests and pray together. Share discovered needs and opportunities for care.

- **ORGANIZE TO MEET NEEDS.** Gather the group's care team to develop a strategy. This includes a plan for communication and response to discovered needs and crises.

- **PLAN AND CONDUCT FELLOWSHIPS, MEALS, AND PROJECTS.** Work with the Friend Shepherd to plan one of each event quarterly. Invite members and friends. Plan conversation and care.

- **MAINTAIN RECORDS.** As requested by the church, maintain, update, and share group records and reports including attendance, contact information, and caring contact results.

- **LEAD TO SERVE.** Enlist and mobilize members to serve in the church and community.

FRIEND SHEPHERD

LEAD THE GROUP TO . . .

- **PRAY.** Pray for the people-group assignment of your group; for lost and unenrolled people; and for group actions to identify, care for, and reach friends.

- **DEVELOP A FRIEND CARE LIST.** Ask for the names of FRANs (friends, relatives, associates, and neighbors) in your people-group assignment, people not enrolled in a group. Develop a plan to pray for and contact FRANs two to four times monthly. Update the list monthly.

- **PLAN AND INVITE FRIENDS TO FELLOWSHIPS, MEALS, AND PROJECTS.** Work with the Member Shepherd to plan one of each quarterly; make events fun and easy for people to get acquainted.

- **ASSIGN CONSISTENT CARING CONTACTS WITH FRIENDS.** Follow up on previous prayer requests; share group event plans; ask how you can pray for the friend and his or her family; and pray together. Report nonconfidential requests. Meet discovered needs.

- **SEND ELECTRONIC REMINDERS ABOUT GROUP PLANS.** To support caring contacts, communicate group plans with friends by email, text, and social media.

- **LEAD TO SERVE.** Enlist and mobilize members and friends to serve in the community and the world.

FOOD SHEPHERD (FOOD/MEAL PLANNER/COORDINATOR)

Fellowship and food go well together with small groups. No matter the setting, adding at least twenty minutes of food and relaxed, bonding conversation is not wasted time.

LEAD THE GROUP TO . . .

- **DECIDE.** In an early session together, ask the group for input about how much food will be provided (meal versus snack).

- **COORDINATE.** Determine who, what, and when. Who is providing what food? When are they providing it? Reduce anxiety by making decisions early and providing reminders.

- **CLEAN UP.** Ask everyone to help for five minutes of cleaning up after the food portion of the time together.

MEET THE AUTHOR

Darryl H. Wilson grew up in Nashville, Tennessee. He graduated from Belmont University (BA, 1982) and The Southern Baptist Theological Seminary (MDiv/CE, 1985 and EdD, 2003). He began teaching Sunday school at age nineteen and responded to the call to ministry at age twenty-one. He served on staff with four Kentucky churches and one in South Carolina.

Since 1997, Darryl has served the Lord and the twenty-four hundred churches of the Kentucky Baptist Convention with a focus on Sunday school, small groups, and discipleship. He began the Sunday School Revolutionary Blog in 2006. That led to publishing *Discipling* (originally published as *Disciple-Making Encounters*) and *Caring* in 2024. Darryl is married to Yvonne. They have two sons and six grandchildren. For fun, he enjoys reading, golf, chess, and traveling.

www.ingramcontent.com/pod-product-compliance
Lightning Source LLC
Chambersburg PA
CBHW070708130626
46553CB00005B/1894